Astrology and Spiritual Develop:

When individuals develop along the lines reflected in their ast
expression of natural potential is possible. Potential is mapp
snapshot of the universe at the time of birth. The birth char
and shows your relationship to the Sun, Moon, and the planets.

You can examine your chart, step-by-step, focusing on each of the issues that impacts your spiritual development. This book begins with the Sun (who you are) and ends with the Ascendant or rising sign (how you present yourself to the world). In between it considers the Moon, each planet, and the Midheaven, revealing how each can become the focus for spiritual energy.

The astrological approach to understanding is multidimensional. It is not limited to any one religion or philosophy. *Charting Your Spiritual Path with Astrology* reveals how your birth chart presents all the possibilities that vibrate within your soul, and leads you to those that are ripe for development.

About the Author

Stephanie Jean Clement, Ph.D. (Colorado), a professional astrologer for over twenty-five years, is a board member of the American Federation of Astrologers, and a faculty member of Kepler College, the only U.S. college or university to offer degrees in astrological studies. She uses her background in transpersonal psychology to help clients define their creative potential and refine their life goals. She is the author of seven books on astrology and one on dreams.

To Write to the Author

If you wish to contact the author or would like more information about this book, please write to the author in care of Llewellyn Worldwide and we will forward your request. Both the author and publisher appreciate hearing from you and learning of your enjoyment of this book and how it has helped you. Llewellyn Worldwide cannot guarantee that every letter written to the author can be answered, but all will be forwarded. Please write to:

Stephanie Clement
℅ Llewellyn Worldwide
P.O. Box 64383, Dept. 0-7387-0114-9
St. Paul, MN 55164-0383, U.S.A.

Please enclose a self-addressed stamped envelope for reply,
or $1.00 to cover costs. If outside U.S.A., enclose
international postal reply coupon.

Many of Llewellyn's authors have websites with additional information
and resources. For more information, please visit our website at
http://www.llewellyn.com

Charting Your
Spiritual Path
with Astrology

Stephanie Jean Clement, Ph.D.

2001
Llewellyn Publications
St. Paul, Minnesota 55164-0383, U.S.A.

First Edition
First Printing, 2001

Book design by Donna Burch
Cover art © 2001 by Digital Stock
Cover design by Kevin R. Brown
Editing by Andrea Neff

Library of Congress Cataloging-in-Publication Data

Clement, Stephanie Jean.
    Charting your spiritual path with astrology / Stephanie Jean Clement.— 1st ed.
        p.   cm.
    Includes bibliographical references and index.
    ISBN 0-7387-0114-9
        1. Astrology. 2. Spiritual life—Miscellanea. I. Title
    BF1729.S64 C54 2001
133.5—dc21   2001038641

Llewellyn Publications
A Division of Llewellyn Worldwide, Ltd.
P.O. Box 64383, Dept. 0-7387-0114-9
St. Paul, MN 55164-0383, U.S.A.
www.llewellyn.com

Printed in the United States of America

Other Books by Stephanie Clement

Charting Your Career
(1999)

Dreams: Working Interactive (with Terry Lee Rosen)
(2000)

What Astrology Can Do for You
(2000)

Power of the Midheaven
(2001)

To teachers everywhere who make a difference,

To Kepler College, where Astrological Studies have found an educational home,

And to my children and grandchildren, who reveal my spiritual path.

Contents

Acknowledgments

I wish to acknowledge all of the people who have made astrology better through their diligent attention to accuracy in calculation and delineation of astrological charts, and to the collection of accurate birth data.

INTRODUCTION

This book is for any person who seeks the inner peace that comes with knowing the purpose for incarnation. It is also for astrologers who are encountering more and more clients looking for answers to existential questions. It provides a systematic look at astrological factors that add up to a spiritually oriented map. The individual who understands this map can move forward through life joyously and courageously, knowing that the path is appropriate to his or her personal beliefs, desires, and needs.

I do not pretend to know what is the proper spiritual path for every individual. How could I? Some days I am not even that sure of my own path. I *do* understand astrology. And I understand a few of the principles that make astrology a vital, powerful, subtle tool for developing spiritual awareness. This book is intended to help you identify the spiritual potential that you were born with, find ways to pursue that potential, and develop strategies for clarifying your spirit and strengthening your mind.

How We Develop

Each of us has the potential to develop along psychic, intuitive, and spiritual lines into that self that best suits our natural gifts. There are essentially three possibilities for how that development may occur:

1. Along the lines dictated by our family, peers, and social milieu: Most of us are taught a set of rules as children. Some of those rules prove to be very useful, and some lessons prove less helpful to our development. Most adults would admit that who they are is largely an outgrowth of their family and culture. Because we live in communities with other people, we need to be adaptable. We can't always have what we want exactly when we want it. Associations with other people provide the arena in which we learn to relate to the world outside ourselves.

2. Along the lines suggested by the individual's conscious mind: Each of us is born with the capacity to learn. If we fail to learn, we die, or we require constant care. Intellect is encouraged by others, but the person inside us is the life and light of the mind. Intelligence can follow many paths, including but not limited to verbal skills, computational ability, artistic flair, and psychic or intuitive understanding. All of these contribute to our development into spiritual beings.

3. Some combination of the first two possibilities; in fact, this is the inevitable path. No one can develop precisely the way someone else dictates. And no one can develop to suit individual desires with no consideration or relationship with the outer world.

When individuals develop along the lines reflected in the astrological chart, the fullest expression of natural potential is possible. Potential is mapped out as a synchronistic "snap shot" of the universe at the time we were born. The birth chart places you at the center of your world, and shows your personal relationship to the Sun, Moon, and planets. Throughout your life, as the planets move forward, new relationships are formed, and these reflect the moments when new thoughts or feelings arise within you, when you are faced with new challenges and opportunities, and when your mind gains new levels of clarity.

The astrological approach to understanding is multidimensional. It is not limited to one religious sect, to one intellectual construct, or to one emotional expression. The birth chart presents *all* the possibilities that vibrate within your soul, and indicates which will be easier or more difficult to manage.

Astrology is based on the methodical process of casting your horoscope—not just your Sun sign, but all the planets and their relationships to each other. It also is the art of evaluating those mathematical relationships and determining their significance for you *as an individual*. No two people are exactly alike, so even charts that are very much alike will be interpreted for the individual being to whom they belong. Through astrology we see the opportunity to consider the whole, using a synchronistic map—a map that reflects the potential and process of each individual.

Each person is in an ideal position to evaluate his or her own astrological chart, gathering pertinent information about what is available in terms of potential (the map) and process (the path). The mission is indicated in the chart, but is only fully understood by opening to your inner spiritual voice.

The developmental paths mentioned above are not strictly independent of one another, but they are distinctly different where dimensional depth is concerned. The first possibility involves care and education by others. Some philosophies suggest that we choose to be born into circumstances that offer the karmic lessons we need to learn. Random events can intervene, throwing us off our karmically designed plan.

The second possibility, simply following the course set by the conscious mind, leaves a lot of room for individual decisions that are subject to factors like:

1. the stage of development at any given time

2. the ability to make decisions based on reasoning and desire (using the ego)

3. experience of how people respond to our actions (conscience or superego)

4. animal instinct for preservation, resolving hunger and shelter needs, as well as sheer comfort demands (the Id)

The third path of development includes the astrological chart. The breadth of personal potential is first and foremost. We cannot ignore the effects of family and culture, the physical limitations of the body and climate, or the developmental limitations of education, language, and training. However, we can seek to understand the roots from which spiritual development can occur by examining the state of the cosmos at the birth hour, and then applying the information gleaned from this examination to the current personal spiritual situation.

The basis for my examination includes the following ideas:

1. Basic goodness exists in the world.

2. We all do the best we can all the time.

3. Each of us has a creative spiritual path.

4. We can make decisions for ourselves.

5. Astrology is a means to delineate individual potential.

We know there has to be a better way to get the gold than by chopping down the beanstalk. How do we let spiritual values become the guide? How can we amplify the spiritual voice so it can compete with the material and cultural voices? In short, how can we make spiritual inclination the first consideration?

Your Higher Purpose

It is important to consider spiritual purpose from the perspective of the Mind of the universe. Not only is it comforting to believe there is a higher purpose, guided by a higher Source, it is also an essential element for your success, for by viewing purpose in this way, any last shreds of egoistic thought can be set aside. You truly can reach a new level of understanding.

Intelligent Activity

There is a particular direction in which your intelligent activity will most likely move. It is obviously where you position yourself and represents your strongest capacities as a human being. At the same time there is a profound instinctual drive to discover meaning, so much so that at some point life without meaning becomes intolerable. Just as physical life is breathed into us, so is the life of the spirit instilled within us.

Your Dharma—Vocational Path

We all accumulate debts and responsibilities on the path toward resolution of difficulties. It is through the exercise of intelligent activity—that is, the use of what we know and how we employ that knowledge—that we even begin to approach the freedom we seek from such indebtedness. You seek intelligent activity in all areas of your life as you face the challenge to rise above merely material considerations.

Finding Harmony Through Conflict

Mediation occurs not only in conflict resolution between or among people; it is an internal psychic function as well. Your principal path or approach to paradoxical problems of all kinds helps you learn about the underlying unity of all things. The capacity to achieve synthesis of opposing ideas and opinions is one example of mediation at work within your mind.

Establishing Factual Knowledge

Concrete knowledge does not stop with scientific definitions of things, nor is it limited to the scientific approach to understanding the relationships between people and things. It also includes a felt sense, an inner awareness of the right relationships between things. You can employ concrete knowledge in the mediation between personality and soul, between physical life and higher consciousness. Only through fusion of these apparently separate facets of your being can you approach true knowledge.

Awakening to Spirit

You can be energetic, even aggressive at times. At other times your energy is directed into thoughtful devotional activities, quieter but no less energetic. Your capacity for dealing with higher spiritual goals is activated through fierce testing. You are subjected to physical, mental, and spiritual demands that leave you changed forever. While duality is part of all experience, there is a struggle that tests even the nature of opposites. This spiritual battle challenges you to rise above merely material considerations.

Psychic Awareness and Compassion

Psychic awareness can be focused to identify the source of conflict and the ground upon which conflict may be resolved. Your higher vision is based on your examination of the essential duality of physical manifestation. One side of duality is the desire or passionate nature; the other side is the innate quality of compassion that comes from another level of experience. The awareness of essential duality is joined with the activity of the mediator to resolve into Unity.

The Union of Wisdom and Love

The path toward fusion of heart and mind, the subjective purpose for manifestation, is perhaps the most central experience of wisdom that you will ever have. Your life's processes are defined. In this fusion you find your transcendent values and learn to apply them each day.

Equilibrium

The search for equilibrium in your life reaches beyond the limits of this plane of manifestation, seeking to integrate the experiences of body, mind, and spirit into one profound experience of unfolded consciousness. This level of integration occurs when the soul and the personality are brought into alignment through accident or through ritual experience. Thus ritual is a valuable path for you as you develop a sense of equilibrium.

Power and Will

Your path to transformation is to integrate power and will to act as a human being. You have the choice of how you implement your will. The power of the universe acts for and with you when your will is tuned to higher spiritual values.

The Birth Chart

The natural arrangement of the signs and houses occurs when zero degrees of Aries, the spring equinox point, aligns with the Ascendant. Each house then has a sign and planet associated with it in the natural chart. The natural placements indicate the transpersonal, or spiritual perspective.

House	Sign	Planet	House	Sign	Planet
1	Aries	Mars	7	Libra	Venus
2	Taurus	Venus	8	Scorpio	Pluto
3	Gemini	Mercury	9	Sagittarius	Jupiter
4	Cancer	Moon	10	Capricorn	Saturn
5	Leo	Sun	11	Aquarius	Uranus
6	Virgo	Mercury	12	Pisces	Neptune

Throughout this book I focus on the planets and the houses naturally associated with them in order to convey some of the underlying spiritual principles that pertain to spiritual astrology.

A second focus is on the sign each planet occupies in the individual chart. Traditional astrologers use the term "accidental" to describe the actual rising sign and the signs that are on each house in a birth chart. The Midheaven, rising sign, and other houses are determined by creating a chart for the exact birth time. Then the planets are arranged in the signs they occupy at the birth time. These placements indicate the personal viewpoint.

When you examine a chart, you can consider the natural associations as a theoretical template describing the state of the universe. The arrangement of the signs and houses in the individual chart is the personal overlay of those same signs and planets, and reflects the individual approach to each area of life. The goal of this book is to help you map the spiritual path, and to see how the geocentric birth chart reflects your personal understanding and inclination toward the spiritual factors in your life.

This book will consider these premises in detail, focusing on specific astrological factors as they affect the creative pursuit of one's individual spiritual path:

Planet	House	Spiritual Context
Sun	5	Spiritual well-being
Moon	4	Core beliefs
Mercury	3 & 6	Communication, mediation, service
Venus	2 & 7	Self-esteem, concrete knowledge, partnership
Mars	1	Devotion to one's life path
Jupiter	9	Transcendent values
Saturn	10	Effective action, career, karma
Uranus	11	Intuition, ritual, equilibrium
Neptune	12	Doubt, resistance, negativity; psychic ability
Pluto	8	Death as a spiritual teacher

CHAPTER 1

THE SUN
Your Creative Potential

The Fifth House, Sun, and Leo describe the basis of your individual path toward spiritual well-being. The Sun is the source of all physical life as we know it. It provides the heat, light, and cosmic energy of our planetary system. It evokes the chemical processes of our carbon-based life forms. Metaphorically the Sun is also the source of our mental, emotional, and spiritual energy. When we are born, we are small bundles of energy that can be defined easily in terms of Sun signs. An Aries baby acts very much like an Aries, while an Aquarian child is very different in basic temperament. As children grow, we see the development of the range of the Sun sign's potential. Development is affected by many of the factors mentioned in the introduction to this book: family circumstances, cultural values, etc. Still, the basic Sun sign characteristics shine through.

So just what are the Sun sign characteristics that indicate spiritual leanings? Let us begin by looking at conscious mental styles from a Jungian perspective. The psychological types of intuition, sensation, thinking, and feeling correspond to the astrological elements of fire, earth, air, and water. They define four principal ways of approaching the world in our daily activities. The Sun sign reveals the basic style of self-consciousness through the elements.

The Sun in the Elements

The elements represent four principal ways we engage in the world. The element of the Sun sign represents the conscious attitude toward the external world. Because the more conscious behavior indicated by the Sun is balanced by the less conscious Moon, it is important to consider them together to get a balanced picture of the psyche. The following descriptions of the Sun (and later descriptions of the Moon) in each element show natural tendencies of thinking style and action. They are taken largely from my book *Charting Your Career*.

The Sun in Fire

Intuitive types listen to their unconscious sources of information, eschewing normal perception. In fact, they are often largely unaware of what is around them in the material world. These people are the inventors, the artists, and the forward thinkers because they can see the possibilities of an idea, often before the means of developing it are apparent. Therefore they pursue what they know the world is not yet prepared for. Intuitives jump to conclusions, but not necessarily without the intermediate steps. They either go through those steps at lightning speed by sizing up an underlying principle or they simply recognize an inevitable match of an idea's potential with their own desires.

Intuitives fit into the educational system rather well, as many high school and college courses make use of the deductive skills intuitives share with the thinking type. You may respond well to the timed testing that is prevalent today. You can master the complexities of mathematics because you can grasp the results without having to ground your learning in some physical way.

Intuitives contribute through their inventiveness. You are generally willing to sacrifice the pleasure of the moment in the hope of greater future achievement. You are also restless and crave inspiration. Because you thrive in situations where getting to the answer is important, you are good at problem-solving and tasks that require ingenuity. Careers in the creative arts, religious inspiration, and scientific discovery all suit the intuitive type. You can become an inspired leader or promoter. For you the game is more important than winning, the chase more interesting than the end result.

The Sun in Earth

Sensation types are primarily interested in practical considerations of the world. They will look at the actualities—facts first. They depend on their five normal senses for perception. They wish to have the experience, not hear about it from others. Sensation types learn by doing, so the learning process may be slower. To be satisfied, they need to go over things carefully. They are not less intelligent because they go slower—they are more careful. When given the time to assimilate information, the sensation type may remember it longer and understand the practical uses in more detail. Studying the theory of engineering may be difficult for the sensation type, but the application is their forte.

You demand satisfaction all along the way, and will not select occupations that lack positive feedback. You are a healthy consumer, loving life and what it has to offer on the material level, and you are best in careers involving real "stuff." You would be a good real estate person, interior decorator, or chef. You enjoy working with your hands and can make this part of your vocation or at least an avocation. You would be a good doctor or health care professional. Any career that requires attention to and intimate understanding of the details is suited to the sensation type.

You generally focus on practical considerations first, and you rely on your five normal senses for perception. You first seek to have an experience, not hear about it from others. You learn by doing, and thus may be a bit slower than some people, but once you know something, you know it forever. You may need to go over things carefully. Once learned, you can apply information to the tasks you set for yourself.

The sensation type's approach to the spiritual side of life is no different. You seek the facts. You want a practical application of whatever you are learning. When contact with the spirit world feels ungrounded, you will find a way to reestablish a level of comfort in the work. You also will not be satisfied with your spiritual work until you can express it concretely in the world in some way.

The Sun in Air

Thinking types tend to be less personal in their approach to the world. They are focusing on an objective truth that they hope to find, and not on the people in their path. They choose to be logical. They choose to be truthful. They choose to be argumentative—after all, they have argued with themselves enough times! They are usually able to go through a thought process once and then stop, without needing to reevaluate. Air types benefit from an education that includes logical training, but they remain one-sided if they skip over the opportunities to appreciate the people and things around them. They judge the world through a logical process that seldom admits consideration of feelings.

Thinking types can do well in careers where it is important to organize and assess quantities of information. You tend to be somewhat more businesslike, able to "cut to the chase" in planning as well as performance. You contribute to society through intellectual criticism, through the exposure of wrongdoing, and through scientific research. You perform well in executive positions partly because such positions are somewhat impersonal. You are willing to tell the truth, even when it is not convenient.

The Sun in Water

If the sensation types say, "Just the facts, ma'am," the feeling types say, "And how does it feel when that happens?" Feeling types evaluate situations on the basis of sentiment and may disregard logical processes as ineffective with others and unsatisfying to themselves. They can think logically, but may choose not to unless pressed by circumstances.

You are not an emotional disaster area. Rather you are prone to making judgments about things, as in, "I feel that is the best way to go." In order to maintain the capacity for fair judgment, it is important to remove or reduce any psychological pollution in the workplace caused by unkind, unsympathetic gossip, threatening behavior on the part of coworkers, or idle complaining that is not backed by constructive suggestions.

Feeling types can do well in careers that call for sensitivity in relating to other people. You have the ability to bridge the gap between people, and therefore make good counselors, sales people, heads of families, members of the clergy—any job where interpersonal relationships are at the core of productive work.

You have a psychic connection to the people and things around you. Often you can "get the point" before other people even state it. You can overreact, but generally return to a more balanced position quickly.

The Sun in the Signs

The Sun indicates your willpower and its direction. One of the reasons we can identify Sun signs in children easily is that they are basically willful in their actions. They are determined, demanding, and rebellious against anything that does not conform to their will. The children of each Sun sign show us the power of will. The following material in parentheses indicates some of what each sign has to learn about the effective exercise of will.

The Sun in Aries

I will be confident (even when what I am doing may be dangerous). I will act (even when waiting would be wise). I will be free (even when obeying others represents a valuable learning experience). I will be assertive, even aggressive (when gentleness may be much more effective). I will argue (when there is no real point in doing so).

The Sun in Taurus

I will be persistent (even after I can see that there is no good reason to proceed further). I will be generous (even when I give away things I truly need). I will be devoted (beyond any logic). I will be possessive (when sharing would gain me a loyal friend). I will persist (even to the edge of doom, even when it is unnecessary).

The Sun in Gemini

I will talk (when I could be silent). I will adapt (when I could be steadfast). I will worry (when I could think things through to effective action). I will be superficial (when I have the capacity to reach profound depths). I will not show emotion (even though I am feeling very deeply). I will do a bit of everything (instead of focusing my energies).

The Sun in Cancer

I will be self-indulgent (when I could take better care of myself). I will be frivolous (when I could be sensible). I will be touchy (when I could be appreciative of another's intention). I will be timid (when I could be expressive). I will be aimlessly dreamy (when I could direct my imagination into fruitful activity). I will procrastinate (when I could allow things to flow in their normal channel).

The Sun in Leo

I will be vain (when I could be magnanimous). I will be domineering (when I could provide dignified leadership). I will be dictatorial (when I could encourage cooperation among others). I will be stubborn (when determination would suffice). I will be snobbish (when I could invite others in, and gain devoted friends in the process).

The Sun in Virgo

I will nitpick (when I could analyze things in a useful manner). I will find fault (where I could just as well find something to praise). I will be skeptical (when I could accept something on faith). I will follow mindlessly (when I could engage my intellect to serve wisely). I will be nervous (where caution is enough).

The Sun in Libra

I will be codependent (when cooperation or independence is better). I will be extravagant (when creative is better). I will be indecisive (when a harmonious decision is required). I will go to extremes (when balance is preferred). I will be temperamental (when assertiveness is enough). I will be vain (when modesty would serve me).

The Sun in Scorpio

I will rebel (when stating my position is enough). I will be suspicious (when being attentive is enough). I will be cruel (when compassion is required). I will be violent (when that is not necessary). I will be stubborn (when tenacity is plenty). I will distrust (when faith is needed). I will go to excess (when moderation is desired).

The Sun in Sagittarius

I will be impractical (when idealism does not require it). I will be dogmatic (when being definite is enough). I will be gullible (when honest assessment is better). I will scatter my energy (when a philosophical attitude accomplishes more). I will gamble (when a little play is enough). I will be self-righteous (when justice needs a bit of mercy).

The Sun in Capricorn

I will be miserly (when prudence is better). I will be secretive (when caution is enough). I will be exacting (when I could be merely conscientious). I will be unsympathetic (when I could exhibit faith in others). I will be pessimistic (when practicality would serve me better). I will suppress my feelings (when self-control does not require it).

The Sun in Aquarius

I will exploit others (when I could be humanitarian). I will rebel (when I might be progressive). I will be eccentric (when I could simply study occult subjects). I will be reclusive (when I could be independent). I will shop until I drop (when I could be philanthropic). I will be logically exacting (when I could listen to my intuition).

The Sun in Pisces

I will be moody (when I could be sympathetic). I will be indecisive (when I could go with the flow). I will feel inferior (when I could adapt to circumstances). I will be secretive (when I only want to be alone). I will soak up psychic negativity (when I could be receptive without losing my balance). I will be indulgent (when I need to be attentive).

Hopefully you can identify some of your childhood traits in the above descriptions of will, and find some of the more adult behaviors in yourself today. Don't beat yourself up if you display the weaknesses of your Sun sign. Instead, use them to work toward the strength of character that is your birthright.

The Sun in the Houses

The house placement of the Sun indicates the individual focus of your creativity. Your impulse on the material, mental, and spiritual levels will be guided into the house where the Sun is found, and you can learn a lot about your spiritual path by considering this fact. If your conscious and unconscious energies naturally go toward one area of your life, then so will your spiritual inclinations. The more consistent your efforts, the more progress you can make on any level of activity.

This section focuses on the part of the body indicated by the house placement of the Sun and develops the physical body as a metaphor for conscious spiritual activity. This may seem old hat to you, or it may provide a fresh new way to relate all areas of your life to your spiritual path.

The Sun in the First House

The head and face are the physical focus for your health and well-being. Injuries and illnesses involving the head affect your sense of self deeply. Whatever lessons come your way, eventually you realize that you only "lose face" with yourself. Vision is the principal vehicle for developing awareness. On the physical plane you may never need glasses, as you tend to perceive the material world clearly. Spiritual vision demands that you see beyond your personal interests. You may become clairvoyant as you develop your spiritual focus.

The Sun in the Second House

The neck, ears, and throat form the physical focus. Hearing is a factor in your contact with the spiritual world, and any illness or injury can affect how you develop spiritually. If you are injured, chiropractic, massage, or other medical treatment can alleviate pain and also help you open to spiritual contacts. Voice is also an important factor. Voice training, either for singing or speaking, can be helpful. You probably express yourself well. Training serves to enhance natural abilities, and allows for effective spiritual expression. You may develop clairaudience through practice. First you need to listen to your own inner voice. Voice training, then, should incorporate a strong component of listening intently to speeches, singing, and ordinary conversation.

The Sun in the Third House

The shoulder, arms, hands, and lungs are the physical focus for your body. You may find that you can feel other people's emotions deeply. You also need to care for your own physical health, as the breath is the source of your capacity to communicate. You take an intellectual approach to life, yet you have tremendous daring when you need it. You are likely to learn through listening to others, and you soak up information wherever you go. You enjoy wandering through the environment, noting the richness of nature and architecture. The more you see and hear, the more sensitive you become to the nuances of the physical environment. Then you begin to hear and see on a different level. Touch becomes a medium of psychic communication for you.

The Sun in the Fourth House

The midsection of your body is where your attention goes when you are working on any creative project, and you evaluate progress by asking if things feel right. The more your conscious awareness focuses on the inner feeling barometer, the more you become aware of the feelings of others and even psychic currents around you. You assimilate data of this kind almost by osmosis. The Solar Plexus Chakra is a spiritual focus for you. This spiritual balance point can be affected by food, emotions, and mental intake. You may need a quiet period after meals or after psychic stress. You can examine and change your core beliefs by facing situations head-on when they are challenged, primarily by males. You find that you function best when you are not struggling in this area. Therefore you may want to do the personal work of self-discovery in the privacy of your own home.

The Sun in the Fifth House

Sometimes you measure the rhythm of your activities against the pulsing of your own heart. You may be able to regulate your heart rate by focusing on your pulse and breath. You tend to engage with the world in a straightforward way, determining what you believe and walking a path that is consistent with your beliefs at all times. Conscious attention to your path leads to each new step in your spiritual life. Creative activities feed your spirit when you throw yourself into them completely. You see the inner childlike enthusiasm in almost everyone, and you thrive in the presence of teachers (and students) who speak and act from their spiritual center.

The Sun in the Sixth House

You benefit from work and other activities in which you can digest and assimilate many ideas before you have to manifest output. Attention to the food you eat can parallel the creative input you receive. You become consciously aware of your path through the digestive metaphor. You "chew the cud," so to speak, of new spiritual ideas, and are not afraid to revisit important decisions when necessary. You mediate between levels of consciousness, and you can be a powerful mediator in your social sphere as well. You seek to purify the spiritual process itself as you move along your path.

The Sun in the Seventh House

The kidneys and bladder form a physical focus for tension. You need to constantly replenish bodily fluids, and should drink purified water to aid the cleansing process on the physical level. Your consciousness focuses on relationships. It is through interchange with others that you find the grist for your spiritual mill. It is also through close contact with others that you find your path. Rarely one to journey alone, you seek partnership in all areas of your life.

The Sun in the Eighth House

Sexual energy is a profound source of pain and pleasure for you. Physical contact with a partner is often necessary for your well-being and health. When you deepen a connection with another person, you transcend your normal perceptions and enter a space where life is illuminated by more than physical senses. Ecstatic experience may first be found in sexual union, but that is only the beginning. You may find that any experience can evoke the memories, the feelings, even the peak of sexual ecstasy.

The Sun in the Ninth House

The hips and thighs are an energetic focal point in your body. Walking, stretching, and flexing the muscles of this area are likely to be part of your daily routine. Your awareness expands as you move. You learn to see and sense anything fresh and new in your environment. You learn to perceive the spiritual source of whatever you encounter. Your spiritual path may take many turnings as you gather the meaningful part of each teacher's lessons to your heart. You can be a powerful teacher if you choose, and you are a teacher for anyone with whom you spend time.

You may find that you focus on spiritual values more than your friends do. Your mental focus is on the nature of life in a more philosophical way, perhaps, so that you are often looking for the higher meaning in events that others brush off as inconsequential. Values that are particularly important to your spiritual path include boldness, loyalty, generosity, and willpower.

You have the capacity to draw on many and varied spiritual disciplines in your development. You will probably try a number of different approaches, but it is through a return to the transcendent values of your Sun sign that you find your strength. Then the soul becomes a mediator between your ordinary material life and creative expression on the spiritual level. As you become the light of your Sun sign, you will retain valuable information and skills from the disciplines you have studied, and you will feel the balance between personal physical urges and creative soul expression.

The Sun in the Tenth House

You may use your knees for purely physical activity, or you may climb the metaphorical corporate ladder. Energy focuses here, and you may find that physical change in the knees accompanies spiritual shifts. You are consciously aware of the connection between practical realities and the imagination or intellect when it comes to effective action. You are able to find the best way to accomplish complex tasks. Effective spiritual action depends on the same kind of assessment. You seek a system that supports your daily work and personal activities, while at the same time providing a container for your spirit and its progress.

The Sun in the Eleventh House

The physiology that supports walking creates a focus on your shins and ankles. You need to stretch and warm up before walking or running in order to prepare your lower legs properly. You need to flex your mental "muscles" before engaging in your work as well. You may choose to play games on your computer, do crossword puzzles, or some other mental activity that you enjoy. Don't save the fun for the end—begin your day with some of it. You have the capacity to join intellect and intuition into a formidable spiritual team. Thought alone is not satisfying, and intuition alone has no ground in fact. You need to cultivate both to satisfy your spiritual yearnings.

The Sun in the Twelfth House

Your feet are the focus of physical activity. It is important for you to have the proper foot wear for whatever sport, work, or other activity you engage in. Support in this area is just as important as comfort. Appearance matters to you emotionally. Your natural empathy allows you see through ordinary appearances. You may be able to see or feel auras around people, animals, and even inanimate objects. Establishing a comfort level with this unusual perception will help you to learn how to "read" it. Outer appearance means almost nothing on the spiritual level. As you become accustomed to what you perceive in others, you come to realize just how important your own thoughts and feelings are to your spiritual development.

Faith, Foresight, and Determination

By choosing the more constructive and creative qualities listed in parentheses in the section "Sun Signs and the Expression of Will," you can overcome the natural tendency to focus only on yourself. As long as you consider only your own personal desires and needs, you are less effective in social situations and you inhibit your own spiritual growth. When you learn to have faith, both in other people and in the universe of spirit, you find that your personal needs often seem to take care of themselves, without much effort from you.

Relaxation of the will is a powerful means to developing foresight. Perhaps you have seen a child with a toy in each hand. When a third toy is presented, the child cries in frustration because it is not possible to keep hold of all three toys. As an adult you learn to have faith that if you set something down, it will not disappear. You will be able to retrieve it when you need it. You gain the foresight needed to delay gratification of one urge in order to serve a larger desire. Then you can aspire to spiritual power.

And it is spiritual power that can drive your determination. A person on a spiritual mission is inspired not only with personal will, but also with the power of acting appropriately, in tune with Mind. You may still make errors along the way, but you are no longer making errors because your focus is only on yourself. Your determination can carry you and the people around you in a more creative direction.

Planets in the Fifth House

Planets in the Fifth House indicate the kinds of people and activities that speak directly to your creativity. They may indicate characteristics of your children, your creative talents, and your general creative direction. They also may reflect recreational interests. The spiritual expression of each planet in the Fifth House indicates how different energies may combine to move you along the path. They either bring key individuals into your life, provide specific kinds of challenges to make you think about spirit, or reveal the conditions under which you are most able to progress. You will find the house position of each planet discussed in the chapter concerning that planet.

Aspects of the Sun

Aspects the Sun makes to other planets show "deep character traits" (Grell, *Key Words*, 1). This deceptively simple phrase in a basic keyword book illuminates the subtlety of astrology. Deep character traits are those that cannot be easily changed, that perhaps cannot be changed at all. Regardless of family, culture, accident, or intention, character is, at its foundation, unshakable.

This does not mean that character cannot be molded. It does mean that we develop according to our own character *in spite* of everything. The inner voice within us will not be denied. It continues to drive us, inspiring us to change and grow. It cannot be eradicated and it never gives up. When we are on a proper path to our true spiritual destiny (whatever that means to us as individuals), the inner voice is a gentle guide. When we stray into less productive territory, it can become more forceful. When we attempt to stifle this inner voice of character, it waits for the proper moment and speaks again. It may have to wait until raging hormones are quieted, and then it speaks. It may only speak through dreams. Yet it can sometimes be seen through random acts of creativity or kindness that seem out of character.

Case Study: Muhammad Ali

Muhammad Ali has the Sun in Capricorn in the Sixth House. The earth element is further emphasized by the Midheaven, Mars, Saturn and Uranus in Taurus, and Neptune in Virgo. Very much a sensation type, Ali forged a career based on his physical strength and skill. His spiritual path has a practical side as well. He has stated that the single most important thing in the world is love, and that he believes we are moving in a direction of greater love and compassion. He was able to follow his spiritual beliefs and still demonstrate his greatness as a boxer. His decision to refuse to be drafted was not only evidence of the depth of his belief, it provided an example for young people who believed the Vietnam War was wrong. Unlike Sonny Liston, who associated with gangsters, and Mike Tyson, who was unable to control his anger around women, Ali only fought in the boxing ring. While he was not a wizard with money, he has talked his spiritual talk and then walked the walk.

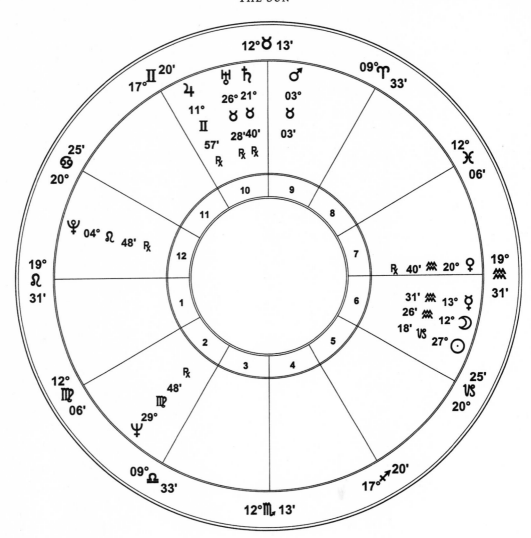

MUHAMMAD ALI

January 17, 1942 / Louisville, KY / 6:35:00 P.M. CST

85W46'00"   38N15'00"

CHAPTER 2

THE MOON
Your Core Beliefs

Much of the pain and limitation we experience is the result of learning, or being taught, so-called truths that are incompatible with our core beliefs. Family and society work together to train us in certain directions, and little is done to nurture our individual realities. It is up to you to identify and nurture the values that are meaningful to you, sifting them from the family history, cultural context, and intellectual resources available to you. When the filtering process is undertaken, you begin to uncover a body of truth that is unique to you. Astrologically, this core of material can be understood by examining the Moon and the Fourth House.

The Moon in the Elements

The Moon reflects the soul. It governs the fluids in the body and imagination in the mind. It generally represents a less conscious part of your being, and reflects the qualities and flexibility of your memory. If the Sun indicates the most likely course of your spiritual path, the Moon indicates some of the qualities of the path itself. It shows, by the element of the sign it occupies, the internal processing that supports your decisions in the outer environment.

The Moon in Fire

Your internal intuitive style is very different from what you show to the world. People may feel the fire of your passion and not know what is behind it. They see you are "fired up" and wonder what is going on. Sharing the fire can be difficult, especially in the early stage where you feel it but don't know the direction it will take.

You often know what will happen, and probably have déjà vu experiences frequently. If you focus on these experiences, you will find that you have them more often than you thought, and you begin to learn how to interpret intuitive or psychic signals more clearly. As you pay more attention, you find that what were once perceived to be anxiety attacks now are signals from your unconscious about present or future events. It is often helpful to share your insights, even in the early stage when you don't have the full picture. By doing this you gain intuitive skill.

The Moon in Earth

There is a practical side to your nature that comes from deep within. On the surface you are not focused on the material side of life, but your inner voice is always presenting some grounded argument that guides your actions. Thus, no matter what you are involved in, there is a considered quality to your actions that generally brings solid results.

Your psychic senses run to the physical. You may be able to dowse for lost objects or water, for example. Or you may find that you sense oncoming illness in yourself and others. To develop this capacity further, you may want to record your psychic sensations and track them. Any time you have communication with your less conscious side, it is important to acknowledge it in some way—to show respect for its power. You don't have to act in every instance, but you can acknowledge that you have received the information. If you don't, the signal may become more distressing, or the voice may sink into silence.

The Moon in Air

Your inner voice is logical—perhaps too logical—and it can have an aloof, cold quality. You may find yourself critiquing your actions in a logical way when your emotional, instinctual, or spiritual response was perfectly suited to the situation. The inner voice can be used to analyze your actions, but you will want to avoid becoming obsessive about every detail of your life. Internal logic is useful in school and other learning situations, as it serves to gather and organize large quantities of material quickly and neatly.

A very real advantage of this inner thinking style is that you may reach a conclusion intuitively or on the basis of feelings, and then examine its logical basis at your leisure. The ability to apply reason to your life—cognitive skills—can help you be socially graceful while also serving your personal desires. You also develop a capacity for delayed gratification of sensual impulses that would not serve your best interests. If an impulse is evaluated and the logic holds up, then you can take action, knowing that you are not violating your internal intellectual standards.

The Moon in Water

You have a powerful internal mechanism for identifying the truth in any situation. You may be able to see auras, and you can certainly feel other people's energy. Because of this you value your privacy. You needed your own room as a child and you continue to need time alone as an adult. Yet you love to know that there are people around you who care about you and respect you as a person.

You tend to judge the world on the basis of your internal meter. You often act on impulse and baffle others by your actions. They don't have any idea where the decision came from unless you tell them. This makes it important to be surrounded by people you trust deeply. Only then can you be yourself. At the same time they will come to trust your psychic sense. On the rare occasion where others attack you directly, you are thrown completely for a loop. Until you understand their motivation, you may be stuck in a loop of trying to figure out what *you* did wrong.

The Sun and Moon in the Same Element

The Sun and the Moon in the elements have been discussed. Now let us consider the combination of Sun and Moon signs as an indicator of your overall thinking style. Together, the Sun and Moon indicate how you approach the world in general, and your spiritual path in particular. The Moon relates to the subconscious or unconscious level of core beliefs and indicates what you have taken into your mind and soul. The Sun indicates both the larger mind of the universe, Unity or God/Goddess as it works through you, and the personal power and will you exert in this physical lifetime. The Sun and Moon work as a team to help you along your spiritual path by reminding you of the values you have at a given moment and stimulating you toward creative change. The placement of the Sun and

Moon in individual elements has been discussed. Next we can examine the situation when both the Sun and Moon are in the same element.

The Sun and Moon in Fire

Your conscious individuality and less conscious interactive style work very well together. The advantage is that you always know your own mind. You intuitively know what is coming and can plan for it on both the spiritual and the material plane. On the outer conscious level, as well as the inner private plane, you may seek the independent path in all areas of your life. You are a strong individual and believe in your own abilities. You have learned to trust your judgment, even when it goes against the logical grain.

The disadvantage of your thinking style is that others will seldom agree with your views. They have their own ideas about how things should go, and they may not see into the future as well as you do. Your task will be to motivate them in the direction you are going by sharing your vision in a useful way. You may be somewhat intolerant of others when they don't see things your way. You may be rather ruthless in your behavior toward them—unable to forget perceived wrongs and thus unable to cooperate fully. The challenge is to use your will to harness the energy inside you and moderate its expression so that others will admire your leadership and choose to follow you.

You have the capacity for the heights of ecstasy and the depths of despair. In spite of a certain volatility, you have strong ethical and moral principles. Thus you can be the consummate bandit, stealing from others "by the book," staying just inside the law. Or you can be a preacher, lawyer, or judge, dispensing fairness according to your own principles. You benefit by using your endless supply of energy in physical activities. You may move far from your birthplace in pursuit of your ideals.

The Sun and Moon in Earth

Your conscious individuality and less conscious interactive style work very well together, and this can be an advantage when practical decisions guide your path. As a child you may have been stubborn in your determination to do and to be whatever you wanted, but that trait develops into a solid, reasonable nature with great power. Able to accept responsibility, your inner personal beliefs are readily revealed to your peers. Your insight into people comes from this capacity to not merely talk the talk, but to also walk the walk.

Your psychic sense of things has palpable reality for you. You may use all the senses to relate to the world—both on the physical and the spiritual planes. Simple activities can trigger visions that are crystal clear, or you may hear conversations that reveal events in the present moment or in the future. Such visions are as real to you as ordinary events. As a child you may have wondered why other people didn't hear or see what you did.

You impress others with your insights. They don't know how you do it, but they respect the fact that you do. Loyalty is important to you for practical reasons. You are, however, loyal to your own principles first. You can change your personal direction when you see trouble ahead, and others may feel left out or betrayed when you do so. You can be somewhat sentimental, and may feel sad when change takes you away from friends or family.

You are open to the practical considerations of spiritual life, but may have some difficulty with the impractical demands of idealism. You focus on mental conflicts and may develop a one-sided perspective, thus limiting your access to spiritual development. By the same token, your ability to find agreement between your practical nature and your inner sense of what is right serves you well in assessing all information gained during spiritual quests. You need to balance your desire for personal control against the potential gain when you are able to relax into changes in the spiritual landscape.

The Sun and Moon in Air

Your conscious individuality and less conscious interactive style work very well together. You can be a romantic in both senses of the term—relishing intriguing personal liaisons as well as hearkening back to earlier times when life seemed more palatable. You tend to be rather nervous and you can take this as a cue that intuition may be coming through. Your inner voice is objective, for the most part, and your outer demeanor reflects this, even if there is internal agitation. Intuition, for you, must be reflected in the external world, or you will opt for the external objective evidence.

You tend to exhaust the possibilities of a situation quickly, perhaps because you are not delving deeply into all the variables, but instead leaping to conclusions. You have a quick mind that sometimes moves from one thought to another before you have gotten to the "meat."

You have to learn to take people as you find them. You are never intentionally unkind and rarely even use harsh words. It may be difficult for others to understand your logic, as it is grounded in your own intuitive premises. You can, however, employ your intellect to analyze others and develop an interactive style for each individual person. In the process you learn to deepen your thinking and extend your mind beyond its present limits.

The Sun and Moon in Water

Your conscious individuality and less conscious interactive style work very well together, as there is a natural flow between your inner life and your outer expression. Your power comes from the strong emotional congruity you express. The advantage of this style is that you rarely disappoint yourself by making ill-considered decisions. In fact, you dislike backtracking and correcting things and prefer to exercise sound judgment in the first place. This decision-making process involves an internal examination of the available facts and psychic input, after which you make a conscious judgment. Only then will you take action. You dislike being pushed into hasty decisions.

You can be suspicious of other people's motives and may test them against your personal standards. This is a disadvantage if you expect others to measure up. You need to remember that they have their own standards, their own intuition, and their own goals.

There is immense creative force in your emotional structure. You have a sexually magnetic nature and find that both men and women are drawn to it. This is not a flaw in your character, and it doesn't mean you will act on every sexual impulse. It is a strength when you use it to motivate others, or when you use it to get your own points across. You must exert an effort of will not to engage your sexual impulses in the workplace.

Your loyalty must be earned, but it is a valuable asset. You enjoy being flattered but recognize flattery for what it is. When you give compliments, you truly mean what you say. You appear inaccessible when you are engaged in an internal dialogue. Because you are usually available, these moments surprise others. However, it is this inner awareness that engenders your deep respect and compassion of others.

The Moon in the Signs

The sign placement of the Moon indicates the qualities of experience you encounter, and the people who can speak for you when you are unable or unwilling to voice your inner thoughts and feelings.

The Moon in Aries

You have a profound belief in your capacity to succeed on your own merits. You connect with people who are willing to explore new beliefs and ideas with you.

The Moon in Taurus

Practical people have the ability to help you systematize your beliefs. They may push you to be more practical, and you have to sort out which of their ideas are compatible with your own spiritual path.

The Moon in Gemini

Communication is one of the surest ways to test or evaluate your beliefs. People in your peer group help you determine which core beliefs are truly yours—they identify patterns that suit your family in general, but don't suit you in particular.

The Moon in Cancer

You naturally understand your beliefs and their source. There is a sense of belonging that follows you even when you are far from home. This allows you to nurture your own and other people's ideals and creativity.

The Moon in Leo

Wherever you are and whomever you are with, you feel like the ruler of your domain. Your self-assurance may cover core beliefs that don't really suit you totally, yet you project certainty and control to those around you.

The Moon in Virgo

You carefully consider your beliefs before you make any changes, examining the history, texture, and value of each one. You understand your past and use it to achieve your practical goals.

The Moon in Libra

You tend to think through each situation that touches on your beliefs, applying a set of logical considerations, including your need or desire to continue in the direction in which you have been going.

The Moon in Scorpio

Change is such a strong component of your life that you are able to abandon any less than useful core beliefs. However, you are careful not to toss away something that has intrinsic value. You analyze your beliefs deeply, based on your contact with other people.

The Moon in Sagittarius

Your core beliefs were good for your family and society of origin, and therefore they may be good for you too. However, you consider changing your mind when those beliefs conflict with perceived reality.

The Moon in Capricorn

You aspire to more ambitious goals than many of your family members. This includes the spiritual path. You apply a very practical measurement to beliefs. If they work, don't change them; if they don't work, replace them. Now.

The Moon in Aquarius

Your typically aloof nature provides a logical, objective method for examining beliefs. You may argue about issues that reveal illogical patterns or constructs, and you calmly and coolly change your own mind.

The Moon in Pisces

Empathy causes you to carefully consider your beliefs, as you don't wish to hurt anyone by taking a radically different direction. However, you also seek the ocean of values that suit your unique values and personal needs.

The Inner Voice

The Moon reflects the inner voice that accompanies you throughout your life. The sign placement of the Moon indicates the kinds of people and experiences that connect you to your core beliefs most directly. The house placement indicates the people who resonate with your inner voice. The Moon also indicates the quality of spirit that seeks to be expressed in your core beliefs. It reflects the portion of the Collective Unconscious—the part of Universal Mind—that is most consistent with your spiritual beliefs during your present lifetime.

The Moon in the Houses

The Moon in the First House

You demonstrate your core values to the world, whether you understand them or not. Since this is inevitable, it is important for you to gain a degree of self-awareness so that you can consciously express the best side of your being, rather than unconsciously expressing values that have been imposed on you.

The Moon in the Second House

Understanding your core values leads directly to increased self-esteem. You thrive when you understand your own motivations and gather them into a useful skill set in career, family, and other associations. Your values become part of your earning power when you understand and embrace them.

The Moon in the Third House

Education is a key factor in working with your core beliefs. Childhood education may impose beliefs that do not resonate with your being, but don't throw them out without examining them for consistency, pertinence to your own life, and spiritual clarity. Then you will be in a position to help other people resolve their conflicting beliefs.

The Moon in the Fourth House

You are centered in your beliefs and are probably comfortable with them. Even if they are not a perfect fit—if some of them have been given to you and you have not examined them—you are probably able to work within their boundaries most of the time. When you contemplate them, you tend to polish the sharp edges rather than exchange them for something altogether new and different. Emotional values are at the heart of your beliefs. Women have influenced your direction strongly, and may have shown you how to make changes without destroying your entire structure of family and nurturance.

The Moon in the Fifth House

You work with your core beliefs in a very creative way. Sometimes you set them aside and "dress up" in different ones. Sometimes you wear your own beliefs like a suit of armor and dare others to challenge you. Sometimes you stir the mix of beliefs, molding the ones that are not a perfect fit into the ones that are truly yours.

The Moon in the Sixth House

More than most people, you work hard to understand your belief system. You examine it item by item, testing each bit to see how it fits logically with the rest. You are able to change your beliefs by first digesting them, then eliminating the residue that does not nurture the rest of the system.

The Moon in the Seventh House

Relationships with significant others form the ground on which you test your beliefs. Business and romantic partners challenge you to grow and change. While this is true of most people, for you it is the heart of your spiritual path, as it allows you to directly confront core beliefs that do not serve your goals.

The Moon in the Eighth House

Your core beliefs are founded in other people's resources. You may depend on others to make your decisions and you believe that they care enough to do so. As an adult you will be challenged to reconsider some of those ideas. You then will be able to use the resources of others instead of being controlled by them.

The Moon in the Ninth House

Higher mind and spirituality form the basis of your core beliefs. You are thus well positioned to pursue your spiritual path, beginning with careful examination of what you learned as a child and continuing as a lifelong educational process.

You experience the bondage to form—the physical body—and you are able to respond to the energies of the earth directly. You can use your will to express through physical form, combine it with the will to know and understand the spiritual realm, and transform instinctual reactions into intuitive responses. You are actually channeling impulses from the collective Mind of the universe. Any conflict you experience is the reflection of the dichotomy between (not the separation of) your physical and spiritual drives. Thus it is imperative for you to experience and understand your physical body on the deepest level possible, as it is the most direct source of your transcendent values.

You tend to focus on the shifting ground of your beliefs. You are not wishy-washy about your values. However, you are willing to change your thinking if evidence suggests the need to do so. You measure your decisions on a feeling basis, listening to your gut re-action to ideas. You can imagine adopting a new attitude without having to test it out in the material world to see if it fits you.

Values that are most likely to impress you on the feeling level include spiritual flexi-bility, the capacity to nurture, receptivity, psychic insight, and finding the flow.

The Moon in the Tenth House

Career and public image are integral to your core beliefs. It may be difficult to separate your sense of self from your public image. Spiritual development will result from care-ful distinction between private and social considerations. The social setting is a worth-while testing ground for your core beliefs.

The Moon in the Eleventh House

Your core beliefs have been strongly influenced by circumstances beyond your family's control. While you may have been surrounded by seemingly helpful people, you have also been introduced to a conglomeration of beliefs that now can bear deeper examina-tion. Use current circumstances to enhance this investigation.

The Moon in the Twelfth House

Institutional patterns have stamped your core beliefs with a nearly indelible set of stric-tures. You need private time in which to consider what remains valuable from the for-mal beliefs your family and childhood impressed on you. Use that time to meditate, read, study, and then evaluate what works for you now.

The Sign on the Fourth House Cusp

The sign on the Fourth House cusp indicates the filter through which you view your core beliefs. The sign reflects the flavor of the most profound resources within you for spiri-tual growth. In fact it is the wellspring of all the best, most creative, and most powerful ideas you will have throughout your lifetime. It indicates the refrain that the inner voice will sing to you when you are sad or filled with joy, when you are pessimistic or opti-mistic, when you are afraid or when you are experiencing the power of love in your life.

Aries on the Fourth House Cusp

The most powerful expression of will comes through Aries, so it is essential that you understand your core beliefs and work through them at all times. When you are able to do this, you provide a charismatic presence and find that you can be tremendously successful. When you don't—when you stray from your own beliefs and rely on direction from others—you stumble and perhaps even fail in your efforts.

To gain a clearer understanding of your own core beliefs, you need to explore the nature of Aries:

1. Learn what it means for you to express your will effectively. Anyone can be willful, like an infant demanding immediate gratification. That style is effective for the baby, but not for you. Explore within yourself for more appropriate expressions of will. Perhaps you focus on sports activities, a musical or writing talent, or the determination to complete scheduled work tasks on time. If you are focused, these tasks will be accomplished cheerfully. You pay attention to the task and not the reward.

2. The creative urge is a strong component of your core beliefs. Whatever you are doing, you need to feel the energy of creativity flowing through your actions. Therefore all destructive acts are and must remain outside the focus of your will.

3. You have a profound understanding of the nature of Unity and will seek it throughout your life. You will find ways to express your understanding of the universe to others, but first you seek to understand and trust it yourself.

4. You understand the spiritual warrior's path. You must lift yourself above the petty battles of the playground of life and seek to express your warrior qualities in the most idealistic way possible—in creative service to others.

Taurus on the Fourth House Cusp

The heart of Taurean core beliefs is desire. As a small child you saw objects and wanted them. You developed skills to get them. You gathered things to yourself as all children do. That is only the first expression of desire. As you have grown, you have developed aspirations—desires that can be sought in the near or distant future. These aspirations include career, family, friends, romance, or anything you decide that you truly want. The key to acknowledging your core beliefs is to understand that the best actions are based on spiritual aspirations and not physical desires.

You, more than most people, recognize that you have a physical body, a physical vehicle for your being. Existence in the physical world requires the satisfaction of basic desires for food, clothing, and shelter. At the second level you recognize powerful desires for friendship, romance, physical love, and personal satisfaction in work, whether in the form of money, fame, or simply self-satisfaction. On a higher level you desire to be fully creative, to leave a lasting impression on the world through your children and your works. Finally, spiritual aspirations are part of your core beliefs. You believe in the power of Spirit. You can find deep within yourself a sense of purpose that goes beyond the ordinary and reaches to touch the sky.

Your core beliefs include an even deeper understanding of the power that is yours. After your ordinary physical resources are exhausted, after you have gotten your second wind from emotional and mental resources, when you feel you have used up every ounce of courage and will that you possess, there arises a third source of will. This source is your soul, the divine element deep within you that provides strength for the occasional struggle that is well outside the limits of your physical being. By cultivating your awareness of this deeper well of energy, you are able to teach the people around you to place their faith in the universe, in God or the Goddess, and not in themselves.

You may feel very alone as you explore your core beliefs, and even as you take action in the world. The challenge is to clarify what part of your beliefs was given to you by others, and what part of that is truly congruent with your deepest beliefs. As you set aside beliefs that don't work for you, you separate yourself from family and friends to some degree. As you gain understanding, you find that you come full circle and can embrace those people again, even though their beliefs are very different from your own.

Gemini on the Fourth House Cusp

Your core beliefs are gathered around the principle of Change—Change with a capital "C" because we are not talking about minor, day-to-day ups and downs. We are considering the profound changes in mind and spirit that lead to human progress. These changes first appear in the beliefs of individuals and may take years or generations to spread throughout human culture, but they are the stuff of material and spiritual progress. You become the mediator between what has gone before and what is possible for the future.

First you must learn how your beliefs allow you to mediate within your own personality. You learn to argue logically and clearly by having internal conversations about questions or problems. You learn to distinguish between what is truly part of your own beliefs and what is not. You see the apparent separation between self and others clearly.

Second, you develop a similar awareness of the connection between mental and spiritual beliefs. Here you experience an adjustment of your personal desires vis-à-vis your spiritual aspirations. You see how the two relate to each other. At this level you may find that you perform the services of a mediator for others.

Third, your core beliefs focus on your relationship to Spirit. At this level you refine your core beliefs concerning your mind, your will, and spiritual love. You find that you lose the personal sense of things and contact the greater Unity and harmony. You may find that you chafe at the restrictions, within yourself or others, that prevent the higher spiritual light from shining forth. You see the spiritual potential in everything, and wish others could see and manifest it more fully.

In the end you discover that you understand both the tendency to struggle or argue, and the tendency to resolution and harmony. As this understanding develops, you also find that you can cheerfully accept other people's foibles, just as you learn to more cheerfully accept your own. You reach a point where mind and heart are expressing as one.

Cancer on the Fourth House Cusp

From the conscious point of view you are certain that your core beliefs are largely instinctual. You may resist the concept that those beliefs have been acquired from family and society at all. When you take a careful look, you find that some of your beliefs are grounded in the material world and the people you have known. Along with those beliefs, you find another, subtler layer of thinking. The symbolism of water is very important to your understanding of your spiritual path. You may be most comfortable when you live near water for this reason.

Life emerged from the water. An examination of the fluids of the body shows that they are like a miniversion of the ocean, replete with the nutrients the body needs to sustain life. Yet you need air to survive. This graphic portrayal of the dualism you experience every day of your life provides a metaphor for the dualism of conscious and unconscious processes. The path to understanding, for you, lies in identifying the two worlds of light and dark for what they are—part of the singularity of Mind.

You may find that at some point in your life your belief system takes a radical departure from what you were taught as a child and what you believed was the proper path for you.

Leo on the Fourth House Cusp

You may find that you resist the teachings of childhood. Family and social interactions have shown you the limitations of accepting what other people say. There lies deep within you the desire to lead rather than follow, and this is true for your beliefs as well as your actions. The direction you tend to take is one of fusion—you look at the varied attitudes of the people around you and join like ideas together, forming an internal spiritual counterpart to the fragmented thinking that seems to prevail around you. What began as a purification of water at some time in your past now becomes a purification by fire. Through this process of self-investigation, you eventually come to understand the divine spirit within you—you achieve true self-awareness. You will be aware of purpose in your life and you will direct that life by designing a plan unique to yourself. Your desire to lead may impel you to teach others what you have learned.

You may find that, while you have a set of beliefs unique to yourself, you also have certain life experiences and skills that influence your beliefs strongly, leading you in a direction other than the path traveled by family members. This path itself has a great impact on the development of your spiritual beliefs and values.

Virgo on the Fourth House Cusp

The essence of your core beliefs centers on the Virgin or Goddess and the fruitful expression of the feminine. You see three distinct expressions of the feminine and, whether you are male or female, you seek to express them through your own life and work. The three expressions are sometimes defined through Eve, Isis, and Mary, as well as other goddesses.

The feminine expression on the mental plane is depicted through the acquisition of knowledge, sometimes through theft. It is the desire to experiment and to understand that is born within you every day of your life. Eve tasted the apple of knowledge, while

Inanna stole knowledge and other precious items from Enki, her father. Brigit and Minerva both have an aspect of learning and the expression of intellect.

Feminine expression on the emotional or astral plane is connected to desire. Isis is remembered as the devoted mother of Horus and the passionate consort of Osiris. Because she was able to gather together the severed parts of Osiris' body, she is revered as the goddess who can overcome fate. In the Hindu pantheon the goddesses are reborn again and again in different forms. An example is Sati, who reincarnated as Parvati, whose dark skin is shed and becomes Kali.

The third expression of the feminine is the cosmic mother. You come to understand that you can be the receptive pole and allow the energy of spirit to act through you. This is metaphorically represented by the process of gestation, in which the sexual poles are brought together to produce new life. You can understand your core beliefs through this metaphor of inspiration. You have the capacity to inspire others to reveal the God and Goddess within themselves because you sense them coming together within yourself.

Libra on the Fourth House Cusp

Your core beliefs center on the principal of balance. More than most people, you understand the illusion of duality. For you, most paradoxes resolve into continua of scales ranging from quality *A* to quality *B*, rather than being perceived as opposites. As the scales tip back and forth you center yourself ever more firmly at the fulcrum point, observing the shifts around you, but no longer participating in the wild swings.

You are not immune to desire. However, at the core you believe that balance is preferable to satisfying the extremes of desire. This belief can be detrimental in interpersonal relations, where most people expect you to express your own desires, and to work with them to satisfy theirs. This is especially true where your sexual nature is involved. It may become essential for you to indulge the extremes of sexual desire in order to have experiences to consider, rather than avoiding sexual acts, and thus having no experience at all.

Sexuality provides a rich arena for you to integrate the male and female principles within yourself. This is a wonderful example of a continuum of variations. If you place masculine and feminine on the ends of a seesaw, the center does not represent withdrawal from sexuality. It represents balance between the two expressions.

Another core belief is that intellect can resolve all problems. You tend to seek logical conclusions for whatever situations arise, and may overlook the physical realities and the feeling component in situations. Just as sexual balance begins with diversity, so may your approach to problem-solving. Even if it be only an intellectual exercise, you may want to consider the physical and emotional realities of a problem as part of the solution.

Ultimately, you have a deep sense of spiritual values. Some of these may have been imposed on you by family and your early childhood environment, and you will want to examine your spiritual beliefs from a number of perspectives, in order to identify those that are truly your own core beliefs.

Scorpio on the Fourth House Cusp

Your core beliefs center on the transformations that occur throughout your life. You have a sense of change and its inevitability, and you may tend to seek change because it is comfortable. The stability of long-term households and relationships may escape you until you identify other principles at work in your core beliefs.

For example, you often feel you are guided on a path, and that change is part of that guidance. You are a "seeker," and you are often looking to the horizon for the next experience even while you are immersed in the present one. While the tug of new experiences is important to your development, it is also important for you to complete each task you are dealt. In this way you resolve karmic responsibility more fully and take what you have learned into the next phase of your life.

As you develop the capacity for contemplative activity, you will find that there can be pauses between experiences. It is in these "gaps" that you are able to integrate your life experience into a package of temperament and skills. If your childhood and family conditioning have focused on the changes very strongly, you will need to cultivate the capacity to tolerate moments when there is little perceivable change. It is in these interludes that you can develop a sense of readiness for the next cycle.

The most fundamental beliefs you have center on desire and its satisfaction. Desire will be experienced on the physical level in terms of sexual and other physical appetites, on the mental plane in terms of ambition, on the emotional plane in terms of fear and anger, and on the spiritual plane in terms of pride. If cruelty has been part of your early life experience, you will need to resolve your issues around this point before you can deal effectively with the others. When this has been accomplished to some degree, then you can proceed with life, making decisions based on your own beliefs, rather than remaining tethered to beliefs imposed by other people.

Sagittarius on the Fourth House Cusp

Your core beliefs center on spiritual aspirations. All the window dressing of day-to-day experience aside, at the core you understand that you are a spiritual being. Early childhood training may have imposed a specific set of spiritual values on you, and these may not be values that you resonate with. A significant part of your path may relate to discovering different systems and digesting the part that is meaningful to you in this lifetime.

You may have focused your energies on intellectual development. This can be very valuable to you, or it can be a trap in which you address the rational, logical side of what you learn, without experiencing the intuitive, spiritual values that underlay just about everything. By the same token, intellectual development provides a substantial ground on which to construct your spiritual value system. A set of values without logical coherence would be difficult to implement.

As your spiritual values begin to provide a one-pointed direction for your life, it is even more important to be certain that these are your own values driving you. And as you press forward you may find that other people, lacking the same kind of focus in their lives, will not appreciate your ability to cut through the unimportant details to the heart of any matter you find significant. They will want to beat around the bush to assuage their own desires—desires that have little or nothing to do with the problem at hand. You will need to keep your eye on your spiritual goal while exercising patience with others.

Capricorn on the Fourth House Cusp

Your home is your castle and it is also the place where you guard your deepest beliefs. One of these is your felt sense of the karmic (or dharmic) path you are on. For you, life is about effective action. If a closely held family belief has practical applications in your life, you will retain the belief despite its inconsistencies or contradiction with other values. This causes you to sometimes appear to be far more rigid than you actually are. Sometimes your actions do not reflect your spiritual beliefs.

You may find a teacher who is able to give you organized instruction to supplement your early childhood education and family values. Such a teacher can guide you through the process of evaluating and discarding values that no longer suit your spiritual path. Even here, though, you must remember that you are the source of your own best instruction where spirit is concerned.

In childhood you tend to respond to the animal and desire nature, basing your beliefs on material matters. Throughout your life you grow into beliefs that address the nature of form and spirit. In the process you reevaluate your beliefs and either discard or reshape them to fit with these higher aspirations. Thus it is out of the earlier attention to desire and matter that spirit can arise and evolve.

Aquarius on the Fourth House Cusp

Highly unusual circumstances conspired to provide an eclectic set of beliefs in your childhood. Your intuition may have worked overtime to provide clues about the future and thus suggest necessary changes in core beliefs. If your parents or family encouraged you to follow your own path, you have thrived on the opportunity, even though you may have stepped off the spiritual path to sample less constructive ideas along the way.

You enjoy the trappings of ritual—it is through ritual that you are able to associate matter and spirit. Whether it be the traditional rituals of your church or religion, or unique rituals you have devised for yourself, the systematic approach to spirit suits you very well. You are generally willing to then state what you have experienced.

Whatever you value receives your best effort. You work hard in your job, you work hard to support and nurture your family, and you devote yourself to service when you are interested in it. Your demeanor may suggest that you are somewhat shallow in your beliefs, yet your intention deepens throughout your life to become dedication, based on your growing self-awareness.

Pisces on the Fourth House Cusp

Being an empathetic person at the core of your being, you respond to the core beliefs of the people around you all the time. However, you need not be a vessel that can only be filled in this way. You are able to draw on your inner instinctual nature and develop your intuition. In the process of this development, you may start out being a psychic medium, subject to the currents of psychic energy around you. Later you develop your intellectual capacity and can then regulate, measure, and evaluate those same psychic currents. When this happens, you become a mediator of the energy instead of being its servant.

You find that you are able to consider multiple beliefs, and you often find the common thread among people's apparently different ideas. Thus you are capable of mediating between different thoughts and feelings very well. As a child the expressed beliefs of your family may have been contradicted by the psychic expressions of the individuals. You had to learn to evaluate those differences early on, weighing what was said against what you could feel. In your adult life you can use this skill set to become a mediator. Further, you are able to discern core beliefs in yourself and others that do not align with each other, and you are able to adjust those beliefs so that they are part of a consistent set of values.

You may feel that you are following a return path to values that have somehow been lost or ignored. Your core beliefs, when you get to the actual core, are probably shared with millions of individuals. If you are willing to spend time peeling away beliefs that have been imposed on you without any systematic method, you can then begin with a solid base and reassemble a more meaningful set of feelings and ideas around them. As this process unfolds you discover your unique position among the multitude of voices.

Planets in the Fourth House

Planets in the Fourth House indicate the kinds of people and events that are most active in the development of your core beliefs. These are the people who live with you, or whose ghosts haunt your self-examinations. They are the events that impel you to look deeper to discover the few things that truly matter to you in this lifetime.

If you don't have any planets in the Fourth House, three possibilities may be explored:

1. The house occupied by the ruler of the Fourth House indicates a part of your life that often takes precedence over your conscious investigation of your core beliefs.

2. Your core beliefs are well established and are not the most important issue where spiritual development is concerned. What you have been taught as a child may serve very well as you explore your spiritual path.

3. You gain the information you need about your core beliefs directly through your own intuition.

In any case, other people will have less influence on your core beliefs than is generally the case. This is a good thing because ultimately you have to rely upon your own inner counsel, but it is a hindrance because you have no one to serve as a measure of your beliefs.

Aspects to the Fourth House Cusp

Most astrologers don't consider aspects to the Fourth House cusp in their traditional delineations. The traditional aspects to the Fourth House are paired by an aspect to the Midheaven. A trine to the IC is reflected in a sextile to the Midheaven, for example. In terms of spiritual path it is very helpful to consider the aspects to this angle as distinct from the Midheaven. They indicate that what is evident in the social sphere (shown by aspects to the Midheaven) is accompanied by feelings and urges that may be quite different (reflected by the IC aspect). For example, Jupiter conjunct the Midheaven often indicates optimism and contentment with events in the material world. It can coincide with success, the start of a new career, or meeting successful people.

At the same time Jupiter forms an opposition to the IC. This indicates a time when you can develop awareness of your own love and wisdom. In the public sphere you find evidence of how the laws of the universe unfold on the social level. You can, at the same time, gain awareness of how your core beliefs have led you to this moment of success. You become aware of your responsibility, even duty, to uphold your values through your actions.

Depending on the aspect set you use, there may not be a complementary aspect. For instance, a septile to the IC is complemented by an angle of 128+ degrees to the Midheaven, and a quintile is complemented by an angle of 108 degrees. I don't know of any astrologers who consider the 128-degree aspect, but some would consider the 108-degree aspect (a tredecile, or 3 x 36 degrees). This is why it is worth calculating the aspects to the IC and considering their meaning.

The Closest Aspect to the Moon

The closest aspect to the Moon indicates an influence that will be felt when spiritual values are undergoing change. The feeling tone of this aspect can act as a signal that your inner voice is speaking to you, urging you to adjust your direction in some way, or simply agreeing with you. How this signal is felt depends on the nature of the aspect and the second planet involved.

Case Study: Muhammad Ali

The closest aspect of the Moon in Ali's chart is a trine to Jupiter. With the Moon in Gemini in the Sixth House and Jupiter in Libra in the Tenth House, Ali was naturally at ease with words. His capacity to deliver little rhyming phrases as part of his pre-fight media persona has given us "Float like a butterfly, sting like a bee," and "Thrilla' in Manila," to name just two. With the Moon in an air sign, Ali used his intellect as well as his physical abilities to move himself through his boxing career. The Moon conjunct Mercury is an indication of the prominence of his verbal skills, and is one indication of how important speech was to his career and to his spiritual process.

The Moon also makes a biseptile aspect to Uranus, suggesting that his mind was quick, his decisions quick, and his physical speed even quicker. This aspect indicates that the talent and physique were only part of the picture. Ali was fated to do the unusual, and to do it with finesse. Once he decided that he would be the greatest fighter, he pursued that goal on every level of his being. Part of his spiritual belief is that we should each become the best we can be, and he devoted himself to doing just that.

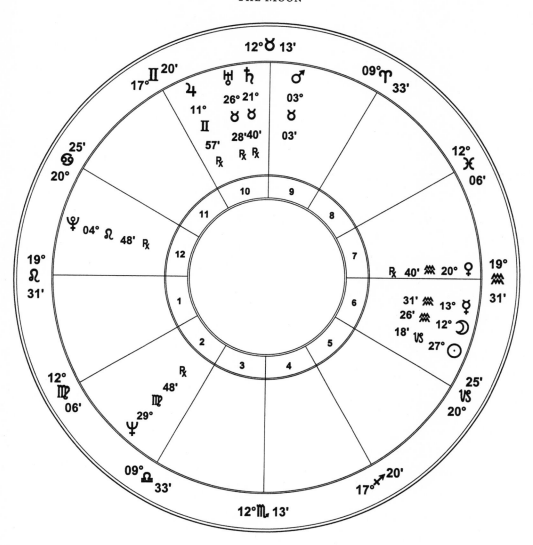

MUHAMMAD ALI

January 17, 1942 / Louisville, KY / 6:35:00 P.M. CST

85W46'00"   38N15'00"

Chapter 3

Mercury
Communication and Mental Development

Most of us have been given a set of "truths" in childhood that we were expected to accept. We were not generally provided with the skills to evaluate what we were taught and to make decisions about what was right for us on an individual basis. To supplement what we have been taught by parents, teachers, and the world at large, we need to develop a spiritual education style that works for us. If we then decide to teach others, we will have a personal track record as an example of the pitfalls on the path of spiritual learning, and we will need communication skills to share these experiences clearly and meaningfully with our students.

Training Your Conscious Mind

Three factors contribute to your ability to train your conscious mind for spiritual development. First, the natural direction of your thinking must be considered. Second, any training should take advantage of this direction, and work with it. Third, training your nervous system, and learning to respond to it, will simplify the process of mind training. Attention to physical and mental realities will prevent misdirection of your spiritual efforts.

Mercury in the Elements

The angel Raphael is associated with healing in the Bible. He was also Tobias' constant companion. The combined capacities for companionship and healing are reflected in Mercury's expression in the elements, and each element reveals a specific spiritual healing path.

Mercury in Fire

Spiritual healing and well-being develop through the conflict between the present and the future. Because healing energy is directed through intellect, you benefit from mental training that focuses on listening to intuition and feelings first, and then seeks ways to confirm that information through logical means. Healing on the physical, mental, emotional, and spiritual levels occurs when conflict is accepted and examined, and then resolved.

Mercury in Earth

Spiritual healing begins on the material plane. Obvious conflicts occur in the arenas of livelihood and physical desire. One of our greatest social problems arises out of the consumption of foods and drugs that do little to engender healthy bodies. You have the capacity to identify and heal illness by directing your intelligence toward proper diagnosis and quality nutrition. You also have the ability to mediate between adversaries and achieve peaceful resolution of problems.

Mercury in Air

Your healing focus lies in words and skillful communication. You use your intellect to examine conflict, discover its significance, and illuminate the path toward resolution. Adept in the technology of communication, you may be able to heal people over long distances. Whether you focus on oral traditions, written word, or artistic communication, you use logic in the mediation between or among people.

Mercury in Water

Your healing style is well suited to the emotional distress around you. You can get into the flow of emotional energy patterns, identifying their disparate components, and guiding others toward calmer, safer modes of expression. You work to illuminate whatever emotional condition you find, not surgically removing an emotional block, but helping bring understanding so that the block relaxes on its own.

Mercury in the Signs

Training the conscious mind involves understanding how you employ reasoning on the conscious level. Spiritual education involves learning how to engage your intuitive function, and intuition is not logical. It is a nonrational function of the mind, designed to help understand the possibilities that lie in the future. Intuition has been thought of as an involuntary function. However, the possibility of training intuition exists. You have a specific way to explore intuition, which then balances the intellectual function.

Mercury in Aries

Your intuition grows when you focus on your intuitive impulse, compare it to what you see around you in the world, and discriminate between what is outside yourself and what is coming from inside. You have the power of observation and the ability to listen to others. Clarity of intuition grows when you accept and work with each insight.

Mercury in Taurus

To develop your intuition, you need to overcome your tendency to hold one-sided views. You have the patience to do this if you work at it. One approach is to always ask what the logical opposite is, and then understand how the two positions are actually part of a continuum, like opposite ends of a seesaw are part of one system.

Mercury in Gemini

Your thinking loves variety and change, and is therefore flexible and versatile. Training may include the cultivation of an orderly approach and honesty, especially with yourself. Correspondence (either orally or through writing) with others is also an important training factor. You need to create a feedback system through which you use inner tension as a signal to focus or refocus your mind. This will help overcome any communication blocks you may have.

Mercury in Cancer

In the material world you nurture and are nurtured by siblings and acquaintances. On the spiritual level you will be able to move others toward their individual spiritual goals by nurturing their confidence. Intuition grows as you pay attention to the needs of others, consciously at first, and later on a psychic or intuitive level.

Mercury in Leo

You have a natural ability to see into the future. What is not always so easy is applying this insight to everyday life. As you apply your awareness of the future, you will develop self-confidence. Your speculations may seem reckless to others. Leadership involves the capacity to build enthusiasm for goals that remain unseen.

Mercury in Virgo

Your digestive system acts as a barometer for your intuition. You feel changes in the material, emotional, and spiritual weather well ahead of time. Instead of simply treating an upset stomach with medicines, use this information to formulate plans and think through strategies.

Mercury in Libra

Your sense of harmony comes into play when intuition arises. You want to fit the new information into what you already know so that you can use the head start it gives you. By knowing the feeling tone of situations in advance, you will learn mediation skills—you have the feelings ahead of time, and therefore can be calm when the moment comes.

Mercury in Scorpio

Your life is filled with transitions—even major transformations. You often feel them coming, and you can use your intuitive senses to make them at least a little easier to manage. Contemplative practice will help clear the mind so the messages are clearer. Then your courage can stand out in the moment of the crisis.

Mercury in Sagittarius

You enjoy pursuing ideas to their logical and/or philosophical outcomes. You cultivate relationships with teachers throughout your life, and you may become a skilled teacher in your own right. Mental training is second nature to you.

Mercury in Capricorn

You are usually very aware of your goals, and the methods most likely to help achieve them. As intuition grows, you also become aware of steps along the future path and how those steps affect both your achievement of the goal and your relationships with other people. This awareness will modify your self-centered ambition.

Mercury in Aquarius

Your inventive nature is well served by developing intuition. You see future needs and focus your thoughts on how to fulfill those needs. Intuition is a natural component of your thinking process. Walking meditation may enhance the intuitive flow.

Mercury in Pisces

You are very receptive to sound. One way to develop intuition is to employ sound in your contemplative practice. This could be simply the sound of your breath, or it could involve chanting, bells, or other musical effects. Listening to someone read helps you relax and focus your mind.

Mercury in the Houses

The house position of Mercury indicates your best communication environment. It also may reflect the qualities of your spiritual teacher.

Mercury in the First House

Your communication is at its best when you are vitally interested in the subject under discussion. Spiritual training is no exception. Choose something that stimulates your enthusiasm and that focuses attention on your internal sense of calm and clarity.

Mercury in the Second House

You make progress when you engage in deliberate activities. Spiritually, this might include calligraphy, Ikebana, or other meditative activities. Your conversational style tends toward focus and brevity.

Mercury in the Third House

You love change, and this may hinder your spiritual development if you skip from one practice to another without engaging in any in-depth practice. A consistent meditative practice can provide an anchor for your otherwise active business and personal life.

Mercury in the Fourth House

People tend to adapt their attitudes to align with yours, but only when you are able to provide convincing reasons to do so. Otherwise they just keep talking until you give in or feel forced to leave the conversation altogether.

Mercury in the Fifth House

You are able to see into the future and to communicate what you see to others. A strong organizer, your contemplative practice can serve to clarify your creative direction and to provide insight in the area of leadership.

Mercury in the Sixth House

Any spiritual practice needs to be a source of knowledge for you. Thus you will want to read, study, and discuss the tenets of the practice. You tend to gain expertise in a narrowly focused specialty, even in your spiritual work. Thus you work best in team situations where each person has specific responsibilities.

Mercury in the Seventh House

Partners are a strong component of your mental life. By talking with a trusted partner, you learn both how to listen and how to speak. You develop sensitivity to others, and therefore sensitivity to your inner voice. Listen first, then determine how to communicate.

Mercury in the Eighth House

You function very well in formal settings, including banks and other financial institutions, any location where funeral arrangements and services are held, insurance offices, and hospitals or offices where surgery is performed. Your best classroom is an arena where your students are practicing what they are learning, and not merely being taught the theory. Another appropriate setting is a place where psychic activity occurs or where psychics work with their clients.

Mercury in the Ninth House

The evolutionary process is sped up for you so that the soul increases in importance and the physical world recedes. This can be difficult, as you live in the physical world and must attend to material needs. As you learn to relate the physical to the spiritual in a creative way, you find that you focus on consciousness itself. The more you do this, the closer you come to full self-awareness that transcends ordinary ego drives. Then you allow a greater Mind to guide your decisions.

You value the ability to communicate on several levels. First, you want to understand the people around you, and for them to understand you. Second, you have an active line of communication with yourself. You can carry on mental conversations in which you test an idea privately to evaluate its logical coherence. Third, you are able to engage in spiritual communication, sometimes even spirit communication via channeling or direct mind transmission.

Transcendent values may include awareness of apparent duality, respect for higher education, discriminating awareness, refinement of ideas, and appreciation of conflict and its resolution.

Mercury in the Tenth House

Your grasp of the practical factors in any situation comes out in your choice of utilitarian spiritual practice. For example, yoga serves both to center and calm the mind and to strengthen and tone the body. Meditation focused on an object is very helpful.

Mercury in the Eleventh House

You see the value of change and even reform in your spiritual practices, yet you also have the capacity for steady thinking and sound judgement. You grasp the essentials of contemplative practice quickly, and then must settle into a consistent daily practice, if only for a few minutes each day.

Mercury in the Twelfth House

You are receptive to energies around you. This is a problem if you take in every idea and feeling that comes your way. It is a strength when you can identify incoming energies and sort through them, attending to those that are important and setting aside less useful or even harmful thoughts and feelings.

Spiritual Communication

Each of us has a direct path by which we can absorb information and put it back out into the world. By sticking to the most available means of communication, you will be able to tell others what you believe and how it affects your life. This skill must be developed before you can become an effective teacher.

On the ordinary level we use intellect to understand a subject, and critical ability to evaluate it. On the spiritual level it is really no different. We have the ability to see through conflicts that arise, identifying the harmony that can emerge from a proper course of action. We often find that we can resolve disagreements, not by providing an answer, but by providing a safe space in which the combatants can discuss their differences. It is possible to use the conflict itself as a tool, instead of viewing it as a barrier.

Planets in the Third House

Planets in the Third House indicate the characteristics of your spiritual teacher(s). Planets here may show something about the religious, moral, or philosophical qualities your teachers possess. They may indicate something about the path your teacher follows.

If there are no planets here, you may be your own best spiritual teacher. Many people are destined for a solitary path, upon which they discover their own spirituality. They do not require one single path or teacher, but many embrace several. Read the section about the house where Mercury is found for information about how best to teach yourself.

CHAPTER 4

VENUS
Self-Esteem, Partnership, and the Spiritual Path

The power of mind is unlimited, except by our own thinking. As we proceed along the spiritual path, self-esteem can grow. As self-esteem grows, progress becomes more certain. The two need each other to move forward. Relationship with another person is a powerful source of energy for the development of self-esteem and for spiritual growth.

Venus has been called the alter ego of the Earth. Very close to the same size, Venus has an atmosphere that is utterly inhospitable to human life. The inner reaches of the unconscious mind were long thought to be inhospitable as well. Modern psychology has delved into the mechanism of mind, and religious mystics have long studied the complex terrain to be found within each of us. The consensus is that to evolve spiritually, we must first look within ourselves. One way to do this is through relationship with others.

Romantic, business, and other relationships all offer us the opportunity to project our thoughts onto other people to see what they (out thoughts) really look like. The more we develop our own consciousness, the more quickly and easily we recognize our own limitations within our portraits of others. The very act of desire for the romantic partner is a projection. The evolutionary nature of relationship allows us to explore our desires and to aspire to a spiritual connection that transcends sexual expression.

Venus in the Elements

Venus in Fire

Your inspirational energy comes from scientific mental activity—you gather practical facts to help manifest love in your life. You are able to discriminate between extremes, and to explore a variety of options in search of the one best way to complete a project. You are able to see the future potential of the loving energy that goes into today's work.

Venus in Earth

You love comfort, and you find you are most comfortable when your somewhat scientific perspective matches your inner sense of propriety. You seek love in your life, not just to satisfy physical urges, but also to create a space in which you can express your intelligence.

Venus in Air

Your intellect is fed through close relationships with other people. These may be romantic connections, or you may connect to people you find attractive for some other reason. Ultimately your spiritual life is enhanced when you are able to communicate what you have learned to others.

Venus in Water

You gather concrete knowledge by talking about the subjects that interest you, and then listening. You like to know the name of everything, and often just the name of an object, a person, or an idea tells you far more than most people learn though more serious study. You use the power of your mind to direct your feeling energy to help others.

Venus in the Signs

The sign placement of Venus in your chart indicates the shading of all expressions of love in your life. The nature of your outlook is colored by all the planets and their placements, but Venus by sign indicates what "spin" you put on your relationships, be they social, business, romantic, or any other. The way you approach relationships has a profound effect on how you gather concrete knowledge and use it as a spiritual tool. Thus it is reasonable to explore Venus through the signs as an indicator of your most likely avenue of approach to other people, one of your best sources of concrete knowledge.

Venus in Aries

When you wish for something, you have the power to manifest it in reality. You are a dreamer, and you are able to achieve your dreams in many cases. You fall in and out of love rather easily, and this includes falling in love with a new spiritual teacher or idea.

Venus in Taurus

You desire to establish a steady course on the path of life, and this includes your approach to serious relationships of all kinds. You recognize the comfort and companionship that can be found in relationships, and you seek steadfast partners. You yourself are faithful, and are therefore conservative in your choice of partners.

Venus in Gemini

Charming and courteous, you make friends easily, and may seem to promise more than you deliver in the long-term relationship department. Your spiritual process is best served by comparable effort in all your relationships, as conflict is not productive. You take a cooperative attitude, and follow through on whatever you promise to do.

Venus in Cancer

You place a high value on home and family, and you may not stray far from your birthplace. You seek harmony in your life and occasionally mistake harmony for spiritual achievement. Harmony is only one aspect of the spiritual path.

Venus in Leo

You thrive in situations where your creature comforts are lavishly cared for. This does not mean you cannot also seek spiritual growth, it just means that you may be expected to demonstrate generosity that you don't always feel. You arouse love, or even devotion, in others.

Venus in Virgo

Your moral boundaries sometimes make it difficult to get close enough to another person to have a strong love relationship. Or you may make practical decisions that fail to give adequate consideration to your partner. The spiritual challenge is to be somewhat practical in an arena that is known for its lack of logic.

Venus in Libra

You know how to blend into any social situation easily, and you are welcomed as a guest. You also have the mind of a general, leading his army into a carefully planned battle. Sometimes your relationships have a touch of both the social and the warrior quality. Focusing on each relationship when you are interacting with the person helps move you to greater spiritual understanding.

Venus in Scorpio

Your physical and sexual intensity can overpower other people who are not ready for the surge of raw power you can generate. You also suffer when you allow your full energy to be released. As you develop the ability to modulate your physical energy, you find that the resulting spiritual ecstasy is a richer experience than simple physical lust.

Venus in Sagittarius

You idealize your relationships, seeking to find love in every contact. You are very sensitive to the desires of romantic, business, and other partners, and can dissipate your energy in trying to satisfy them. You benefit from solid, grounded partners who help you remain focused, and from them you learn how to contain and use your idealistic intuition to good advantage.

Venus in Capricorn

You pay close attention to the results of all your activities. If things end up "done," but done badly, you are not satisfied. You learn more from your own experience and from social contact with older or younger people, and less from peers.

Venus in Aquarius

You are well suited to the environment of team activities. You can focus on your own role while maintaining a sense of the larger drama. Your progressive views on the subject of romantic partnership may contradict what you were taught as a child. It is probably more important to make sure those ideas do not run against the current of your spiritual leanings.

Venus in Pisces

You have a deep longing for meaningful love relationships in your life, and you may tend to give in to others in order to gain such a relationship. Because you are very impressionable, you will find that careful investigation into any new project or relationship will save you a lot of trouble.

Venus in the Houses

The house placement of Venus in your chart indicates an area of life that amplifies your capacity for acquiring concrete knowledge. We are each capable of learning in diverse arenas, but there is one area where our learning is poignant and profound. As a reflection of your alter ego, Venus reveals, by its house placement, the lessons that will stick with you along the path and serve you best in your overall education.

Venus in the First House

Not the sort of person to buy into anyone's program totally, you think your way through whatever you are studying, and that includes spiritual matters. Only when you have gathered knowledge about the subject of your studies and processed the facts will you be personally satisfied.

Venus in the Second House

You recognize that your spiritual self-worth is very important. You like to have nice things around you, and will not deny your material desires too much. At the same time, you choose studies and other activities that are consistent with your metaphysical goals.

Venus in the Third House

You gather knowledge about your spiritual connections wherever you find yourself. Always looking for information to guide your progress, you listen to others and evaluate what they say, then decide for yourself. Siblings can be a strong influence.

Venus in the Fourth House

Women focus your attention on the social values that underlie your beliefs. They show you that it isn't just about you, but includes broader interpersonal significance. Awareness of the nurturing component of interaction is key to your learning process.

Venus in the Fifth House

You often experience strong physical attraction to other people, which could be mistaken for romantic love, but which may also be the result of pure magnetism. You can increase your knowledge very quickly through contact with any person who has this intense attraction for you.

Venus in the Sixth House

You are able to gather knowledge in on-the-job situations, and you benefit from strong, well-defined team involvement. While you recognize the difficulties of romance in the workplace, you are sometimes strongly attracted to coworkers and may have to sort out complicated feelings in order to accomplish your work.

Venus in the Seventh House

You make friends quickly, and you fall in love quickly. You thrive on strong partnerships with both sexes, and you may form lifelong partnerships with both men and women. You thrive in social settings. Each relationship or event provides you with the grounding you need for spiritual work.

Venus in the Eighth House

Concrete knowledge comes through transitions. Death is an important spiritual teacher for you, as it teaches you how to manage the feelings associated with profound changes in your life. Spiritual transformation evokes some of the same feelings.

Venus in the Ninth House

You anchor your higher values in concrete facts. Your life includes many significant events in the social sphere where you are able to gather information concerning whatever is truly important to you. You may have learned certain manners from your family and teachers, but it is in the interaction with others that you learn how to be both a considerate companion and a responsible individual. At first you may be indulgent, doing whatever the "crowd" suggests, or flirtatious regardless of the risk involved. You may vacillate, letting others lead you into activities that are not in your own best interests. As you move through your life, you attend to your own values early in any relationship. There is less friction in your interaction with others, and you find that others appreciate your ability to define and adhere to your principles. Knowledge comes from many sources, and you are able to learn from the experience of others. You may travel the world to gather information, or you may stay closer to home and read about far-reaching ideas.

Venus in the Tenth House

You are quite capable of using your magnetic attraction in your career and public life, and you do this without confusing sexual interest with your other goals. You may find that alliances with older individuals help you early in your life, and that you later form alliances with people much younger than yourself.

Venus in the Eleventh House

Your progressive views concerning love relationships may be an outgrowth of contact with people you have known in past lives, and with whom you had different relationships from the one you have now. You learn best in situations where you have some independence, yet you appreciate the security of strong relationships of all kinds.

Venus in the Twelfth House

Your strong desire for love can sometimes overrule your judgment. You are impressionable in the bargain, and learn more than you intended to from close interactions with other people. This can be a fast path to spiritual awareness if you establish a level of self-control on the physical plane.

CHAPTER 5

NEPTUNE
Doubt, Resistance, and the
Development of Psychic Ability

The spiritual path has a number of pitfalls. Some problems are posed by other people, but some of the most treacherous lie in our own minds. The Twelfth House reflects our private thoughts, which sometimes become our own prison, trapping us within walls and bars of our own making. These may be the karmic result of the past, or they may be the result of our contemporary actions. This is the house of secrets, doubts, and negativity. It is also the house of privacy, reserve, and receptivity.

Let's approach these potentials in pairs. Privacy and secrets are both part of the Twelfth House continuum of experience. Even children love the feeling of independence and power that comes with a secret. Adults often structure their lives around issues of privacy. Traditional households once had both a workshop and a sewing room, and each was the private domain of Dad and Mom. Social etiquette requires that the bathroom door be closed when occupied. Adoption agencies often require that each child have his or her own room. Problems only arise when the secrets we keep are detrimental to ourselves or to others.

Doubt and reserve share a similar continuum. Some people are shy and withdrawn because they believe they cannot compete on a par with their peers. Some people are simply reserved. They feel no need to jump in first, and prefer to watch and learn from others. Each of us nurtures our own inner thoughts. We face the challenge of sorting out ideas and feelings that are provoked by outside influences, or that arise from the unconscious, more or less unbidden. Among our unconscious materials we find content arising from the collective Mind. This information may be bizarre and frightening, and we may not have a structure in place to deal with it. Without input from other people we may not be able to manage this input, and more doubt about our abilities can arise.

Self-doubt keeps us from moving forward. How does the mechanism work? The mind is made up of conscious, memory, and unconscious components. Neptune reflects attributes of the secret, the unconscious, and the conscious mind. This planet reflects both the territory of the unconscious and the process through which unconscious material emerges into consciousness. It indicates the personal pathway between levels of mind.

We store experiences in the unconscious. To the extent that the storage process itself is conscious, the contents are retrievable on a regular basis. See chapter 3 on Mercury for more information on learning and memory processes. Probably ninety percent or more of what is stored is simply taken in without any thought. For example, we seldom think about taking the next breath, or about the exact nature of the pattern formed by leaves falling from trees, or the shape of the post that supports the stop sign at the next corner. We associate sounds and smells with early childhood memories that we could not retrieve through our usual thinking processes.

When a situation causes us to doubt, it is largely because the present situation is incongruent with what we have learned in the past. The moment has come when we want something new, and we evaluate the good reasons for wanting to change. But in the unconscious there is turmoil. We feel naughty, anxious, reluctant, or undeserving. No one is going to punish us yet we resist following our own hearts. We are unable to move forward.

Resistance is what happens between what we had before and what we want for the future. It can be as simple as having our cake and eating it too. It can arise as a dilemma—we want to change and we know what the first step is, but our fear or doubt keeps us from taking that step. For example, you may be very certain that you have found the right life partner, but you fail to move to the next level in the relationship because you "know" your parents wouldn't like this partner.

Doubt is made up of more than personal experience. It incorporates ideas you have heard from people you trust. It is a distillation of what you have read, both fiction and nonfiction. It may include memories of situations that have very little in common with the current problem. This kind of resistance can keep you from the very things that are most attractive, most beneficial, and most needed.

Resistance is not all bad. We need to have consistency in our lives. If change were so easy, we would have no stability—we would be wandering through life with no security. Without resistance we could be talked into all sorts of actions that could harm us and others. We need to consider alternatives when we make decisions. What we need is a way to identify the resistance for what it is, and then find ways to work with it. Where your spiritual path is concerned, Neptune reveals how doubt arises for you, and also shows a viable process for resolving resistance. The sign associated with the Twelfth House indicates your initial response to doubt and resistance. This response develops into more suitable strategies as you work with your spiritual growth. One such strategy involves your psychic ability.

Developing Your Psychic Ability

First I want to define psychic ability in a very specific way. Psychics claim all sorts of powers: the ability to see and hear at a distance (clairvoyance and clairaudience), the ability to "feel" or "sense" the conditions surrounding others, the ability to contact the deceased, and the ability to move physical objects without using anything but the power of the mind (telekinesis). I intend to define psychic ability without getting into any of these specific applications.

You use your psychic sense to understand the world of the present. Psychic senses are adjunct to the ordinary senses, and may metaphorically mirror any of them. You may feel that you actively choose to use your psychic senses. Often people just "get an impression" of some kind. Most people don't see auras, but many people can "feel" energy emanating from another person. Certainly they can feel the heat of the other person if they are close enough. Some people occasionally see a sort of halo around other people, particularly in certain lighting situations.

To develop your psychic ability means to become more aware of these subtle nuances of sensation that seem unexplainable by ordinary methods. Neptune is one indicator of how you can develop this ability. By developing your psychic awareness, you will find that you connect to the earth and to other people in a different way. You learn about connections to everything and everyone, and you then see increased importance in developing and maintaining your spiritual values.

Neptune in the Elements

The best of desire rises to the level of selfless devotion, and the best of psychic sensitivity rises to the level of compassion. The element in which Neptune is found defines generations according to their capacity for selflessness, and how they arrive there. The following chart indicates the years when Neptune enters each element.

Fire	Earth	Air	Water
1806	1820	1834	1847
1861	1874	1887	1901
1914	1928	1943	1955
1970	1984	1998	2011
2025	2038		

Neptune in Fire

The fire of physical desire can be transmuted into passionate devotion to the spiritual path. You may be tested more than once in this area, as the physical body is both a necessity for life and an anchor for material and emotional desires. Your higher aspirations tend toward the future, and because of this your actions in the present are enthusiastic as long as a positive goal is in sight.

Neptune in Earth

Elevating your desires to the soul level involves first paying attention to your needs and desires on the material plane. Sometimes you may confuse need with desire, believing that more of something is better. The material lesson to be learned is moderation in all things, including moderation. An occasional excess need not hinder spiritual development. In fact, the person who understands his or her desires is well ahead on the spiritual path.

Neptune in Air

Your imagination may provide rich material for satisfaction of your desires. Without direction, however, imagination keeps you so busy that you don't get to the task of thinking through what is most important to spiritual progress for you. Meditation that focuses on the breath may be good, as it focuses on the mechanism of communication at the same time. Interchange with other people in writing or orally helps you pin down the structure of your spiritual aspirations.

Neptune in Water

Your capacity to flow with the spiritual current is great. So is your capacity to go with the flow of peer pressure, demands of your job, and physical appetites. During your life you may experience the streaming of energy associated with rising kundalini energy. By following this energy through each of the chakras, you eventually reach a state of spiritual balance in which you can become aligned with your true spiritual mission.

Neptune in the Signs

Neptune in Aries

As a small child you really don't experience resistance. You simply jump into everything that attracts you. This somewhat reckless approach is not a problem as long as you don't injure yourself or feel restricted by the people around you. But a child needs to resist the urge to chase a ball into the street when a car is coming, and an adult needs to be sensible about taking medications in the right dosage.

There is a contemplative side to the rash energy of Aries. Passion never builds if we don't learn to anticipate. Once I planned a trip with my mother—just the two of us. Unfortunately we were never able to take that trip. My mother told me that she was not terribly sad, as more than half the fun had been in the planning. Just because we cannot have what we want at the exact moment we want it does not mean that we cannot continue to move toward the desired goal, or enjoy the process itself.

It is important for you to acknowledge your sudden impulses, even if you don't take action. By noticing your desires, you honor your personal process. Then you can consider how to move toward the goal. The development of patience will be a key focus for you as you make changes in your spiritual beliefs. First you have to be patient with yourself.

Then you have to develop patience in dealing with family and friends who may not understand why you wish to make certain changes. Then you need to be patient with your role models, who inevitably will reveal their shortcomings. Finally, you have to be patient with the goal itself, which is ever changing and developing.

Neptune in Taurus

As a child you may have wanted to hold on to what you had with a strong grip. You wanted things to "stay put" in your life. You have organized your life around a set of principles that permit movement within a secure structure. You may even take pride in the fact that your private life is not in constant turmoil, like some of your friends.

Resistance is experienced in the nature of that stability. If you are bound to the relative security of your life, you may resist change, even when it is practical and desirable. It is important for you to understand that the most profound changes come when you allow the structure of your life to open to something new. The paradox is that on one hand you seek stability, and on the other you have intense desires. Desire, by its nature, implies some degree of change. You want to add something to the mix of what you already have. Doubt arises when you try to decide what to let go of.

Your spiritual path includes the task of acknowledging your desire on the material level, identifying your spiritual aspirations, and exerting your will to find a balance between the two. You will not be able to give up physical desires as long as you are in the body. They are part and parcel of what it means to be alive. Your inner voice will not let you ignore your spiritual aspirations, as they are every bit as much a part of you. Strength of will determines your progress. The willful desire of a child to hold on to every toy can be transmuted into spiritual will that both holds on to what is valuable from the past and sets aside things that no longer serve your spiritual aspirations.

Neptune in Gemini

You have a tape recording in your mind that plays itself without your approval. It is comprised of scripts that have been instilled in you by family and teachers, and by yourself. The scripts are designed to remind you of those precepts of your education that have come into play in the past. Everyone has some of these tapes. Yours may keep you from making fresh decisions based on current information.

For example, you may have a tape that basically says, "I won't like you anymore if you do that." You no longer recall who the "I" was in the first place, but you hear the tape. It doesn't really matter who first said this to you—the tape simply plays. In the moment when you are trying to make your own decision, that tape is not helpful. It creates doubt that limits your own growth.

If you hear a tape like this, ask why, in all seriousness. Then listen to the answer. "Because I say so" may have been an appropriate answer when you were three years old and "I" was your mother. As an adult, however, your own conscious intelligence is more useful. You are now seeking an answer that is fully conscious and meaningful to the challenge of the moment.

By asking a question of the internal tape, you then allow a moment for clarity to arise. You begin to see how the influence of others has affected you, and you learn to work with your personality urges and your spiritual desires—you become a mediator instead of simply reacting to those tapes.

Neptune in Cancer

Your childhood family experience provides a basic trust, and perhaps a basic fear, of the dynamics of the nurturing process. You are sensitive to the nuances of your own upbringing—in fact, you may be hypersensitive to issues surrounding family, the loyalty you owe to family members, and the disappointments caused when parents and family fail to follow through as expected or promised.

Your yearning for satisfaction of desires through the nurturing process can only be satisfied by you. No one else can fully understand your desires and completely fulfill them. However, once you attain a level of self-satisfaction, you can immediately begin to nurture others, identifying their needs, distinguishing need from desire, and providing what is best for the other person's spiritual growth.

You have to have a very open heart to fully understand another person. An open heart is not a drawback for you because it serves to inform you about your own deepest desires as well. Sometimes you will be drawn to help another person because what that person needs is the same as what you desire. By helping the other person, you also fulfill your own desire on the most profound level of emotion and spirit.

Neptune in Leo

Your psychic senses are tuned to the future. Often you come up with ideas that other people cannot grasp, as they are more focused on the present moment. When you meet the frustration of not getting your ideas across, not getting the funding for a big project, or not feeling your warmth returned by other people, you may tend to exaggerate your position to get agreement. You only set yourself up for disappointment when you push too hard. It is better to regroup and redefine your goals so that your associates can relate to what you are asking for.

Your leadership depends on your capacity to serve up your plans in palatable units. Your enthusiasm need not be diluted in this process, but it may need to be harnessed. Development of your psychic ability will serve you well. As you learn to see through outer appearances and words, you come to understand the true material desires and spiritual aspirations of the people around you. Then you can focus your own aspirations to match the ambiance, thereby matching the desires of the people around you. If you do this well, others will follow when you take the lead, and your enthusiasm will transfer to them. Psychic information may be felt in the area of the solar plexus and heart as an expanding warmth or constricting coldness.

Neptune in Virgo

You understand people at the intuitive level, but may find that their outer actions baffle you. While you can be completely logical, the psychic information you obtain may need to be examined fully before its internal logic is revealed. Your interest in healing certainly extends to the emotional, mental, and spiritual healing that many people are seeking. You may find that this healing inclination arises in the spiritual realm and seeks grounding in the material. You have the capacity to heal, but only when you have completed a thorough self-examination and removed the blinders of your own ego.

When you consider your own behavior, you may notice that nagging others arises from an internalized message about your own behavior. Obsessing over details may reflect behaviors you learned in childhood. You internalized these behaviors more or less unconsciously, but you can now examine them and begin to set them aside in favor of more positive communication styles. As you learn to be more generous with yourself, you find you relax around other people. As you curtail your nagging behavior with others, you find that you are generally more satisfied with your own efforts.

You will always be able to resurrect attention to detail and critical awareness when they are useful or necessary. What you leave behind is the demanding, obsessive quality that only limits your success.

Neptune in Libra

Your psychic sense is directly connected to intellect. Whether you hear, see, or even smell psychic information, mental processing reveals the meaning. It may help to share psychic insights with others, as this is the way you can identify your own projections and distinguish them from psychic energy being projected by other people.

Language is a powerful medium for your peer group. During your lifetime several profound changes in communication have occurred, including the rise of personal computers and the Internet. These allow you to communicate instantly with points around the world. This does not lessen the desirability of psychic development. Being able to reach out may actually enhance psychic ability, as you can confirm your thinking quickly and easily in many cases.

You may want to record your psychic impressions in a journal. In this way you can track and confirm your impressions later. Too often we dismiss these impressions and may miss the connections. The psychic undercurrents of your life provide a rich resource for your imagination, and they reveal how your life is a fabric woven of various energies.

Neptune in Scorpio

There is always activity in the deepest recesses of your mind. You feel movement well before it emerges from the subconscious so you can examine it in the light of day. Your instincts have always been good, and you may occasionally want to kick yourself for ignoring them.

Your interest in the psychic realm can be fostered through the study of different kinds of psychic work. When you find methods that resonate with you, they are easily learned and even easier to apply. Experiment with dowsing, psycho-kinesis, and telepathy. Look into astrology, Tarot, numerology, or other methods of forecasting. Try several styles of meditation to see what works best for you.

The best path for you is to find a combination of approaches that works for you. No one teacher will be able to give you everything you need. As you develop a package of psychic skills, you find that any self-doubt recedes into the background. You will still probably question yourself from time to time, but your ability to extend your awareness into your present surroundings, as well as into the future, will serve to strengthen your self-confidence.

Neptune in Sagittarius

You often know things before other people get their first clue. You are well positioned to take advantage of this advance information and may thrive in environments where being a bit ahead of the game is important.

You also are adept at considering the facets of a problem deeply and thoroughly before taking action. You are willing to read up on a subject, interview experts, or perhaps discuss the topic with like-minded friends and family. If someone you respect is enthusiastic about a new field, you will learn all you can about it.

Whatever your interests, you always find a way to fit them into your larger worldview, and that includes the spiritual plane. If something doesn't fit, you either work to find a way to make it fit, or you eventually discard it. Until you develop this capacity for discrimination, you go from one thing to another without any apparent direction. In the end, however, all these threads will tend to come back together, and whatever is not useful will be set aside.

Neptune in Capricorn

You have a psychic connection to your solid material surroundings. You "see" how to manipulate the environment to suit your needs, and you may feel or see ley lines in the earth. Dowsing for water or other purposes can be developed. You can identify sticks, dowsing rods, or other implements that "feel" right in your hands, and perhaps find someone who is adept to teach you.

You can enhance your ability significantly by using the principles of Feng Shui and magic in the arrangement of your living and working environments. Most of us benefit from proper arrangement of our surroundings. You can use your practical intelligence to both beautify your space and energetically align yourself and your possessions.

You may also spend time researching and exploring religious questions as part of your spiritual quest. Not one for surface examination, if you do take on a religious or spiritual study, you will study the profound depths of the subject before you are through.

Neptune in Aquarius

The strong focus on electronic media in your lifetime reflects the social openness of the times. You are able to move in different social circles because you are open to the energies of people who are different from yourself. You attract people at least partly because you are open yourself, but you also have a magnetic, perhaps even charismatic, personality.

Doubts can arise because your thinking is so different from that of your parents and grandparents. You are susceptible to influence from others, and you may want to consider the ideas of your peers carefully before you discard your family and social heritage completely. Contemplative practice can help bring balance when you are being drawn in a new direction very quickly.

Your capacity for personal change allows you to experiment and then adopt new spiritual beliefs. It is important, once you take on a new belief, to explore it deeply. Your own sincere effort is what is needed to make spiritual progress. Intellectually, you know there is no "quick fix" in the spiritual department.

Neptune in Pisces

You are tuned to the currents of psychic energy around you, and you can see your way through dramatic social and environmental changes. Because you are so sensitive, you need to develop ways to insulate yourself from ideas and feelings that run counter to your personal beliefs.

By following emotional themes in your life, you discover both the deep historical roots of your thinking, as well as the contemporary psychic fads or trends. Hereditary and social roots provide stability and distance from the whims of the moment. Then you can more safely examine the current trends toward self-realization among your friends and acquaintances. Drugs and alcohol will never be suitable means to achieve spiritual growth for you, and could cause trouble if you indulge in them. Besides, you can easily learn to meditate, to use creative visualization techniques, and even to channel spiritual beings.

Neptune in the Houses

All of us can cultivate receptivity on the emotional and psychic levels. Your peer group shares many of the same abilities that you discover in yourself, but you will find that each person has one arena in which he or she excels when it comes to how receptivity facilitates creativity and imagination.

Neptune in the First House

You tend to doubt your own abilities, especially at first. Yet you have a glow around you that other people find very attractive. You have the capacity to be open and unselfish, especially if you first address your own doubts and begin to dispel them.

Neptune in the Second House

You have a way with design. Your furniture always seems to be in the right place, both on the physical level and on the spiritual plane. You will find that alcohol and drugs do little for you, and will want to manage even prescription medications very carefully.

Neptune in the Third House

Your impressionability makes you a great storyteller. In the process of reading everything you can get your hands on, you will discover avenues for your spiritual development that are quite different from the traditional family values you grew up with.

Neptune in the Fourth House

Power issues in childhood caused you to develop some strange, possibly conflicting, core beliefs. As you gain personal strength, you are able to challenge these ideas and resolve them to suit your own needs and desires for transformation.

Psychic, intuitive, empathetic people in your childhood reveal the inconsistencies of your core beliefs and can provide resources to help you change them, or the fortitude to stick with them for the sake of others.

Neptune in the Fifth House

All creative activities, but especially children, open your heart to fuller expression of your creativity. Pay attention to your psychic sense, as it leads to a richer experience of your environment, and fuels creative efforts.

Neptune in the Sixth House

Your understanding of people and situations comes from an internal source. This awareness can develop into healing ability, perhaps through massage or magnetic touch. You are often willing to extend yourself toward others without reservation.

Neptune in the Seventh House

You are idealistic about partnership and love. Through strong relationships you are able to pursue your spiritual path. Weak relationships can lead to serious disappointment. Therefore you will want to use your head as well as your heart when you enter into what you expect to be a long-term union.

Neptune in the Eighth House

You are connected to the world of shamanism and magic through a deep personal understanding of death, birth, and other important life transitions. You may be able to feel big changes well ahead of time, and use this sense to plan ahead. You also feel the texture of other people's emotional and material resources, and thus learn just how much you can ask of them.

Neptune in the Ninth House

Single-minded purpose is necessary for you as you seek transcendent values. On the physical level you are all too sensitive to the influences around you. This sensitivity can become a mystical tool for understanding the true nature of duality. You need a heart connection to your spiritual work—you have to get past the mental work and get to the intense connection that many people find in their gurus. You may find that refining your mental processes is essential to support the focused attention to your chosen path.

Neptune in the Tenth House

Even in crowds you can tune your psychic abilities. At first there is a clutter of input that is confusing at best. Over time, however, you refine your directional awareness and can track individuals through the busiest markets, or identify the one person who needs the emotional support you have to offer. You may be a skillful manager, as you understand the way to motivate others.

Neptune in the Eleventh House

Group situations draw out your psychic sensitivity, and you may tire easily until you learn how to manage the flow of psychic energies. Group dynamics fascinate you and you have a charismatic touch that can fire up the crowd around you. You can identify circumstances that require your psychic touch; the rest of the time you can let your awareness simmer on the back burner.

Neptune in the Twelfth House

Your doubts come from deep within you and are connected to your past—in this life-time and in others. You are able to understand past connections in other people, too. You can be a direct channel for spirit messages, transmission from distant points, and subtle messages from people close to you.

Planets in the Twelfth House

Planets in the Twelfth House have just risen over the horizon. They have a quality similar to the Sun early in the day. They cast their influence on you in a fresh, genuine expression of their energy, just as the Sun provides new light and warmth each day. You accept this energy secretly. You gather it to you for consideration, but you may not discuss it with anyone until late in your life.

Both your doubts and your psychic strengths are a reflection of planets in the Twelfth House. They serve as guideposts along the path of self-discovery. Your doubts may center on the qualities these planets represent. Your teachers may exemplify the qualities of these planets to the extent that they reach your inner psychic core and help you understand your potential. In the end these planets indicate qualities that you can bring out of yourself and carry into the world to help others, and the feelings of compassion surrounding all your activities. If there are no planets in the Twelfth House, the planet associated with the sign on the cusp indicates where you tend to resolve doubt and resistance.

Case Study: Muhammad Ali

Neptune in Virgo in the Second House reflects Ali's ability to see deep into the character of his opponents. Part of a Grand Trine with the Sun and Uranus, Neptune reflects the basic condition of psychic awareness that Ali showed throughout his career as a boxer. Even more significant, however, is his deep understanding of his own self-worth. Some saw his refusal to join the army as a rejection of all that America stood for. The youth of the nation hailed him as an icon—a martyr to the cause of a generation of people who no longer felt constrained to fight a war just because someone told them to do so.

Ali mustered a lot of courage to make this decision. He really had no way of knowing how long he would be in jail for his beliefs. Yet he gave up what was probably the peak of his boxing career rather than violate his own beliefs. Whether we agree with him or not, I feel we can admire his devotion to his values.

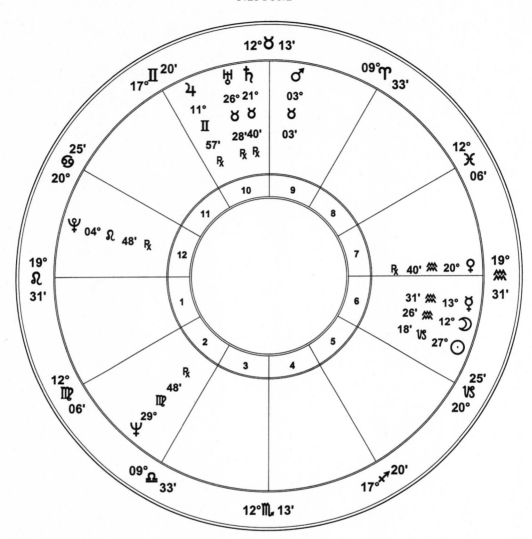

MUHAMMAD ALI

January 17, 1942 / Louisville, KY / 6:35:00 P.M. CST
85W46'00" 38N15'00"

CHAPTER 6

PLUTO

Death and Transformation as a Spiritual Process

Pluto, Scorpio, and the Eighth House in the birth chart deal with issues of death and transformation. On the spiritual path the shaman must undergo a deathlike initiation in order to come into his or her shamanic powers. In fact, we have continual experiences of death to the old way of being and birth to new possibilities.

I am reminded by my personal experience that, while I have made some progress on the path, I can fall back into childhood reactions when I am surprised by transformative events. I like to think I am above such "childish" behavior, but I am not. What is the spiritual lesson in such events?

- They are signposts to indicate our general progress. I don't act like that all the time. I try to change my behavior as soon as I notice a pattern that I judge to be deficient in some way.

- They signal a need to be gentle and kind with myself. I am human after all. I cannot be perfect, and my childhood experience is a deeply rooted part of myself.

- I must make friends with these personal realities in order to move forward. I must accept my behavior as part of me. It is not all than I am, however, and I don't need to feel bad (naughty) when I fail to respond in a way that my adult self finds acceptable.

- No one understands the child within me the way I do. I am the best source of support and encouragement for the inner child. Change can occur if I allow the child in me to work through the unattractive behavior to a fuller understanding. Perhaps I did not have that opportunity when I was little, but I have it now. I can empower myself to change, not by denying or ignoring my behavior, but by accepting it.

The Eighth House in your chart delineates the mechanisms for self-acceptance and change that are most available and appropriate for you in this lifetime. By understanding them you can develop a sense of self in the present and a set of behaviors that lead more directly to your goal. And you can understand and discard behaviors from the past that no longer serve you in your journey on the spiritual path.

The Sign on the Eighth House Cusp

The sign on the Eighth House cusp indicates the background or stage on which you make all of the major changes in your life. It colors your attitudes and suggests the best transformation forum for you.

Aries on the Eighth House Cusp

You want to get to the business of transformation. You have probably had an intuition that change was coming, and you may tend to rush through the actual moment of change. You understand the new possibilities that follow any change and you want to see and experience them. When you are stopped in the middle of a transformation process, you may find the philosophical or spiritual examination extremely uncomfortable. As a child, all that discussion of possibilities left you stranded on a sidetrack of information that meant nothing to you personally. Yet you believe that the philosophical approach is worthwhile. It just isn't your style. It doesn't evoke courage within you, and it lacks the boldness of decision that characterizes your transformation process.

Taurus on the Eighth House Cusp

If you stubbornly resist change in your life, you will constantly find yourself against the wall with nowhere to go. Transformation is of the essence of your life, more than most people, because you have the capacity to be up against the wall, hugging it for dear life for quite a while before you discover the doorway right in front of you into the next phase of your life. You simply need to release the latch and walk through.

Once you get past your stubborn attachment to having the path be exactly as you had planned it, you find that your intelligence leads you to express love for other beings and for yourself. When this happens, you act on the soul level and you no longer need to hold on to an idea, a material possession, or an emotion. Then each transition becomes an opportunity instead of an obstacle.

Gemini on the Eighth House Cusp

Whenever you are at a point where change needs to occur, you find that cosmic energy pours into your heart, body, and mind. You are filled with the capacity to move ahead to something new, and you may inadvertently leave others in your wake. You learn to bring them along with you, or reconnect later. You use your thinking capacity to mediate among the opportunities that come to you. You use it to mediate between other people when they disagree. It is through careful thought that you make progress, and it is your ability to think through a situation that provides the greatest potential for spiritual transformation.

Cancer on the Eighth House Cusp

More than most people, you connect to larger change processes. You may even be able to feel the earth's rotation when you lay on the ground and watch the stars. Yet your most skillful interactions occur in small groups or one-on-one situations in which you use your nurturing abilities to smooth the path for transformation.

You are able to see the light within other people and to nurture it. This spiritual capacity also works in your own life to transform your mundane ideas into spiritual aspirations. Because you are able to stimulate the spiritual motives in other people, you make a strong leader, but you are not likely to be the most public figure. Rather, you guide others and share in their successes without stealing their glory. You see yourself as part of the whole process that leads to success.

Leo on the Eighth House Cusp

While change and death may cause emotional upset, you usually come around quickly to a state of mind that allows you to help other people who are sharing the crisis with you. You take a leadership role by first assessing your own feelings and dealing with them, then acting compassionately toward others. This capacity can take years to develop, and still you feel like a child occasionally when you are stressed.

Virgo on the Eighth House Cusp

Your adult transformation process is grounded in examination of details, but in an analytical, not emotional, way. You seek to understand a situation fully, and you may wonder why others can't see the reality you see. When a situation occurs that is outside your capacity to grasp the details, you tend to take one of two paths (or you may even try to take both paths at once). One path is to sort of laugh it off, making light of what may be a serious problem. The other path is to engage in conversation that is designed both to elicit the information you need and to draw upon your own flexibility and the adaptable capacity of the other person. You feel split into two parts when you do this, and later go back to the Virgo examination of the situation to understand what has happened. You often need to think things through on your own before making final decisions.

Libra on the Eighth House Cusp

Your path toward self-transformation involves balance. You may be dismayed when your best efforts cannot soothe situations and feelings. When you are provoked, you tend to fall back on childhood patterns. Common ones include splitting into two styles of communication, or taking a paternal attitude toward the people involved. Both of these techniques may work in given situations, but they may not feel satisfying to you. You still desire to find that balance point within yourself. It may be helpful to identify which of your typical responses you favor, and try the other one instead. In this way you make friends with both and integrate them to achieve the desired balance. If you can do both—communicate clearly and take a paternal attitude—then you may be able to salve the feelings of others and communicate your intention at the same time.

Scorpio on the Eighth House Cusp

The direct path to change is always a good choice. Your strong awareness of the rhythm of change matches your will in such situations. Death is seen as a natural adjustment or companion for life. When major transitions occur, you tend to face them and enter into them with all your faculties alert. Open to the experience, you feel the joy or sadness, anger or fear of the moment in the moment.

Sagittarius on the Eighth House Cusp

You are philosophical in your thinking, and you are able to make changes more smoothly when you are in in a contemplative frame of mind. Sudden or unexpected events can throw you back into childhood feelings of being threatened. When you feel that way, it is hard to act like a rational, thinking person, and you may revert to what feels like a life and death struggle for independence. In comparing the two choices, you naturally desire to act the adult, meditating about the changes you need to make, and planning how to achieve them.

By experiencing both the philosophical and the threatened feelings, you develop compassion for others. When they feel threatened, you can take a philosophical position and act as an anchor for their difficult experiences. Paradoxically, when you feel threatened, you allow them the opportunity to perform up to their level of philosophical development. In both cases, by going with your own experience, you are able to help others.

Capricorn on the Eighth House Cusp

You are constantly striving to reach the top—in career, relationships, sports, or whatever activity you engage in. When you reach the top, you may not be satisfied, and then you descend from your pinnacle and begin to climb another mountain. Often your experience of transformation revolves around your perception of the descent. You naturally feel less elevated during the transition, and you may find that you feel angry, even when you have begun the change process yourself. You second-guess your own decisions and may strike out at others.

However, you always come back around to your own intelligence. Transformation may not follow a gradually ascending path for you, but you definitely attain the heights and depths. Oddly, it is in the depths that you find the courage and strength to work with others. Without the experience of the downside of life, you would not appreciate what other people are going through, and therefore could lack compassion.

Aquarius on the Eighth House Cusp

Your stage for transformation is set with the trappings of intellect. You like to think through a process to its logical end before you make decisions. If you don't have enough time to do this, you tend to make absolute decisions that don't leave any room for flexibility. Such decisions, if examined carefully, will reflect the same feeling that you had as a child when adults made decisions for you. There is a sense of being trapped in an invisible cage. You may not feel out of balance, but you fear that any movement may cause you to fall from your high wire.

While you may wish to be independent in all things, feeling stuck is a cue to ask for help. By asking you will feel less isolated. The act of extending your hand to another person for help will get you moving again. I am reminded of learning to ride a bicycle. Someone has their hand on the bike to steady it, and that hand provides the confidence we need to experience the balancing technique as we pedal. Before we know it, the hand is no longer there and we are balancing just fine.

Pisces on the Eighth House Cusp

Your stage is set so that you can maintain your reserve. You don't want your change process out there for everyone to see. You like to think you have inner composure that can overcome emotionally agitating obstacles, and it is important to you to reflect that composure in your outer demeanor. When caught off guard, you revert to childhood patterns. You may have been overwhelmed by the burden of responsibility you bore, and power struggles with others may have colored your experiences. Or you may have learned early on to cultivate a sort of dreamy hopefulness in the face of whatever came your way. If you find, as an adult, that you respond much too forcefully in a power struggle, you may be dismayed at the emotionality of your outbursts. Acceptance of that emotional inner child provides the first step on the path to true inner tranquility.

Pluto in the Elements

The sign placement of Pluto identifies the alchemical element that is most active in a chart where transformation is concerned. This placement reveals how you naturally relate to death and other changes in your life and suggests the clearest path to personal transformation. Even if Pluto is the only planet in an element, it still represents the power you have available when facing death or other changes.

Pluto in Fire

Your most direct way of managing transformative events is to will yourself to envision the future. Whether this means imagining life without someone who has left you, or simply moving from one home to another, your strength lies in the ability to listen to your own intuition.

Yet you also sense the hand of the divine—however you define divinity in your life—in the unfolding of a larger plan. While in the moment of transition you may feel helpless and weak, you don't remain helpless for long because you quickly begin to evaluate clues about outcome. You gather information from your surroundings, your thoughts, your feelings, and your sense of spiritual connection to the energy around you.

Pluto in Earth

Potentially more matter-of-fact about issues concerning death and change, you take transitions in stride for the most part. In the occasional instance when a death or change catches you off guard, you may feel that you are unable to move out of one feeling into another. When you feel stuck, you may need to gather your will to take some action. By focusing on simple, practical details, you take steps, one at a time, to lift the weight of feelings that have mired you temporarily.

Generally you are able to handle the details of planning that are required when death or change occurs. You grasp the practical need for one thing to die before another may be born, for example. You also may be profoundly aware of past-life events or the potential of a future lifetime, and you find practical ways to bridge the apparent gaps between the two.

Pluto in Air

Language becomes your medium for dealing with transitions. You think through the feelings in the moment, and can benefit from sharing your thoughts with others. You also are able to find the right things to say in a crisis, helping others think through the change process.

You are able to gather disparate threads of information together into a meaningful pattern. Often when changes seem random or illogical, you find links that provide the comfort and security you need. You can speak intelligently concerning the deeper meaning of transitions because you place each event against a larger backdrop of history and culture.

Pluto in Water

You have the innate capacity to engage feelings that are appropriate to the nature of events. If you have been discouraged from expressing those feelings, you may attempt to bury them deep within yourself. This is not helpful in the long run because the feelings resurface later or eat away at you internally.

What works better is to find suitable ways to express your distress, fear, anger—even your joy. This involves having the conscious experience of feelings and evaluating them for yourself instead of suppressing them. While this is no easy task, it is possible for you to become a stable rock in the midst of a river of change. You have your feelings *and* continue to manage the tasks before you, and you may surprise yourself at how well you handle even severe traumas.

Pluto in the Signs

Because Pluto moves so slowly, people born twelve to thirty years apart may have this planet in the same sign. Your parents and children, however, may have a very different focus for their thoughts and feelings concerning death, and also concerning how to exercise personal power in all areas of life. The following section lists people who have Pluto in each sign, and also inventions that were developed during that time.

Pluto in Aries

The last time Pluto was in Aries was between 1823 and 1853. Some people born at that time include Leo Tolstoy, Jules Verne, Emily Dickinson, Helena Blavatsky, Edouard Manet, Ramakrishna, Edgar Degas, Andrew Carnegie, Mark Twain, Grover Cleveland, William James, William McKinley, Sarah Bernhardt, Thomas A. Edison, Alexander Graham Bell, Jesse James, and Wyatt Earp. Inventions credited to this time period include the sewing machine, mechanical reaper, digital computer, Braille writing, the bicycle, and the bunsen burner.

Pluto in Taurus

The last time Pluto was in Taurus was between 1853 and 1882. Individuals born in that time frame include Vincent Van Gogh, Sigmund Freud, John Philip Sousa, George Bernard Shaw, Woodrow Wilson, Arthur Conan Doyle, John Dewey, Billy the Kid, Pierre Curie, Alan Leo (English astrologer), Rudolph Steiner, Edith Wharton, Swami Vivekananda, Henri Toulouse-Lautrec, William Butler Yeats, Warren Harding, Henry Ford,

Wilbur and Orville Wright, Marie Curie, Frank Lloyd Wright, Alfred Adler, Nikolai Lenin, Gertrude Stein, Winston Churchill, Albert Schweitzer, Rainer Maria Rilke, and Llewellyn George. Inventions include the gatling gun, dynamite, the typewriter, the dental drill, the telephone, the phonograph, the filament light bulb, and the incandescent light bulb.

Pluto in Gemini

Pluto was in Gemini from 1882 to 1912. Births during that period include Benito Mussolini, Harry S. Truman, Sinclair Lewis, Isak Dinesen, George Patton, Chiang Kai-Shek, Boris Karloff, Arnold Toynbee, Nehru, Hedda Hopper, Katherine Anne Porter, Rose Kennedy, Henry Miller, Pearl S. Buck, Mae West, Paramahansa Yogananda, Nikita Khrushchev, Rudolph Valentino, R. Buckminster Fuller, Amelia Earhart, Norman Vincent Peale, Al Capone, Duke Ellington, Humphrey Bogart, and Margaret Mead. Inventions include the motor car, the motion picture camera, the diesel engine, wireless radio, the cloud chamber, the vacuum cleaner, the biplane, the electrocardiograph, and the teleprinter.

Pluto in Cancer

Pluto was in Cancer from 1912 to 1939. Notable births include Burt Lancaster, Albert Camus, Gypsy Rose Lee, William Burroughs, Arthur Miller, Jackie Gleason, Eugene McCarthy, George Montgomery, John F. Kennedy, Phyllis Diller, Indira Gandhi, Gamel Abdul Nasser, Ann Landers and Abigail Van Buren, Thelonius Monk, Ray Bradbury, John Glenn, Rocky Marciano, Virginia E. Johnson (of Masters and Johnson), Gore Vidal, Queen Elizabeth II, Marilyn Monroe, Allen Ginsberg, and Carl Weschchke, owner of Llewellyn Worldwide. Inventions include the television, iron lung, cyclotron, radar, and the binary calculator.

Pluto in Leo

Pluto was in Leo from 1939 until 1957, and a bit after that when it retrograded back and forth. Births include Fidel Castro, Janet Leigh, Eartha Kitt, Shirley Temple, Martin Luther King, Jr., Audrey Hepburn, Jacqueline Kennedy Onassis, Grace Kelly, Arnold Palmer, Neil Armstrong, Johnny Cash, Elizabeth Taylor, Yoko Ono, Ralph Nader, Shirley MacLaine, Sophia Loren, Elvis Presley, Carol Burnett, Ken Kesey, Bill Cosby, Peter Fonda, Grace Slick, Muhammad Ali, Paul McCartney, Ringo Starr, George Harrison,

John Lennon, and Prince Charles. Inventions include the modern digital computer, the kidney machine, the nuclear reactor, and contraceptive pills.

Pluto in Virgo

Pluto was in Virgo from 1711 to 1725 and again from 1957 until 1972. Notable births include Frederick the Great, Christoph von Gluck, Immanuel Kant, Jean Jacques Rousseau, Mike Tyson, Tom Arnold, Princess Diana, and Sharon Stone. Early inventions include the mercury thermometer. Modern inventions include the silicon chip, lasers, microprocessors, pantyhose, and Barbie dolls.

Pluto in Libra

Pluto was in Libra from 1725 to 1737 and again from 1972 until 1984. Famous births include Casanova, George Washington, Joseph Haydn, Captain James Cook, Catherine the Great, Patrick Henry, John Hancock, F. A. Mesmer, Daniel Boone, John Adams, Monica Lewinsky, Michelle Kwan, and Shaquille O'Neal. Early inventions include the ship's chronometer. Modern inventions include the compact disk, personal computer, live polio vaccine, and the CAT scan.

Pluto in Scorpio

Pluto was in Scorpio from 1737 to 1748 and again from 1983 until 1995. Famous births include Thomas Jefferson, Thomas Paine, Benedict Arnold, Madame Dubarry, Francisco Goya, Jon-Benet Ramsey, and Prince Henry of England. Early inventions include the Leyden jar. Modern inventions include cold fusion, Viagra, web browsers, networking computers, and rollerblades.

Pluto in Sagittarius

Pluto was in Sagittarius from 1748 until 1762. Pluto is in Sagittarius at the time of this writing, and will remain in this sign until 2008. Famous births include Goethe, Louis XVI and Marie Antoinette, Mozart, Lafayette, William Bligh, George Rogers Clark, Kamehameha I, Aaron Burr, Charles X, William Blake, James Monroe, Noah Webster, Robert Burnes, and Friedrich Schiller. Early inventions include the spinning Jenny and the sextant. Modern inventions include animal cloning.

Pluto in Capricorn

Pluto was in Capricorn from 1762 until 1778, and will be there again from 2008 until 2023. Births include Andrew Jackson, Napoleon, Empress Josephine, John Jacob Astor, William Wordsworth, Ludwig van Beethoven, Samuel Taylor Coleridge, and Jane Austen. Early inventions include the flush toilet and the submarine.

Pluto in Aquarius

Pluto was in Aquarius from 1777 until 1798 and will be there again from 2023 until 2043. Births include Daniel Webster, Washington Irving, Jacob Grimm, Davy Crockett, Lord Byron, Percy Bysshe Shelley, John Keats, Franz Schubert, and Mary Shelley. Inventions include the hot air balloon, the electric cell, power loom, threshing machine, steamboat, cotton gin, and lithography.

Pluto in Pisces

Pluto was in Pisces from 1798 until 1823, and will enter this sign again in 2043. Notable births include Honoré de Balzac, Alexander Pushkin, Ralph Waldo Emerson, George Sand, Elizabeth Barrett Browning, John Stuart Mill, Edgar Allan Poe, Abraham Lincoln, Charles Darwin, Charlotte Brontë, Emily Brontë, Queen Victoria, Walt Whitman, Herman Melville, George Elliot, Mary Baker Eddy, Clara Barton, and Ulysses S. Grant. Inventions include the electric battery, punch cards, the gas lamp, the glider, steam locomotive, the safety lamp, and photography.

Pluto in the Houses

Pluto moves so slowly that it remains in the same sign for entire generations. One way to distinguish the influence of this planet is to consider its house placement, which changes much more quickly. Even though Pluto moves through the signs very slowly, it can be found in any house in the chart. The house placement of Pluto reflects how you approach the use of power and will in your life. From the spiritual perspective it shows the area of your life in which you tend to respond most strongly to transformation.

Pluto in the First House

Your personality often initiates changes along your spiritual path. Thus it is important for you to consider how you appear to others, as their response is a key to understanding the transitions in your life. For example, if other people become agitated or angry each time you make a change, you may be coming on too strong for the situation, or at least too strong for those individuals. On the other hand, if your intervention brings calm to difficult situations, you can figure that you are showing compassion while also handling the situation itself.

Pluto in the Second House

Issues of self-esteem may push you toward transformations in your life. Material success can lift you out of material poverty, and it may improve your sense of self-worth, but it is your understanding of the flow of spiritual energy that has the biggest impact on your spiritual development in the long run.

Pluto in the Third House

Your concern for siblings and peers is a strong force for spiritual change. You may be strongly influenced by what they say and do, and through experience you learn how your willpower engages in the change process. Thus you find that by watching and listening, you learn how other people use their power. Then you can exert your own will more consistently and compassionately.

Pluto in the Fourth House

Change comes from deep within your being. The inner voice guides you—and not always in calm, quiet ways. You tend to act only when you are certain that you can—or must. Thus you sometimes have stored up enough energy to explode like a volcano. To be more compassionate, both to yourself and toward others, you gradually learn to exert your will sooner so that you no longer explode out of control. Power issues in childhood caused you to develop some strange, possibly conflicting core beliefs. As you gain personal strength, you are able to challenge these ideas and resolve them to suit your own needs and desires for transformation.

Pluto in the Fifth House

You find the appropriate change mechanism by engaging wholeheartedly in creative efforts. When you do this, the act itself impels you toward transformation. Others may see changes in you before you are fully aware of them yourself.

Pluto in the Sixth House

When you are busiest, you are also the most capable of transformation. Serving others opens you to spiritual development, and working for yourself positions you on a progressive path. Both are essential to effect positive change in your life. You develop the capacity for change by using your will to push through difficult situations in the work environment, or through health problems.

Pluto in the Seventh House

Your keen awareness of others is integral to how you make changes. When you focus on yourself, you can get stuck, but when you focus on significant people in your life, your energy flows more smoothly. You find the juice of compassion in the exchange of energy with others. Then you handle changes with greater equanimity.

Pluto in the Eighth House

One change begets another in your life. You see transformation as a way of life, not an isolated event. Often you feel changes coming long before any outward signs are visible. You dwell in the underworld of the mind. Without training you are susceptible to the energies of people around you, and you fall under their spells easily. With training you can cast your own spells, and certainly you can use your power to protect yourself. You have tremendous endurance—your ability to keep going means that you can chart a spiritual path and make definite progress. You tend to be around when traumatic events happen to other people, and you may have your own share of difficulties. These experiences place you in the ideal spot to help others, as you know how they feel and you know just how to lift their spirits.

Pluto in the Ninth House

As you pursue your transcendent values, you will find that death has no hold on you. You take the shaman's path by going through the darkness. You may feel that you have succumbed to sexual seduction in the past, but don't beat yourself up over that. Sexual energy is a source of powerful devotion and motivation. As you gain understanding of the values that matter most to you, you will find that ecstasy, while beginning in a sexual expression, actually reaches spiritual heights that erase the barriers of the body. As a shaman you are able to lift others out of their physical death experiences into the healing light you understand as Spirit. You sense the power of transcendence in yourself and others. You move from learning about transformation within yourself to healing and helping others who must experience rapid, dramatic changes.

Pluto in the Tenth House

Change begins for you when you first feel the tug of ambition—you want something more or better. As you deal with transformations, your goal-oriented behavior becomes spiritual aspiration rather than simple material seeking.

Pluto in the Eleventh House

Circumstances impel you to change, ready or not. Sometimes you feel you must listen to a lot of other people's dreams and follow them. It is important to weigh their urgings against the inner voice of your own desire.

Pluto in the Twelfth House

Death has played a large part in creating doubt about your abilities. Use private time to examine your present knowledge and skills, and you may find that confidence replaces doubt. You need quiet moments to build your power.

Planets in the Eighth House

When planets occupy the Eighth House, they indicate the presence of strong influences in the area of spiritual transformation. The house of other people's resources, the Eighth House indicates what kinds of people lend their spiritual resources to you as you travel your own path. Planets here also indicate the nature of any death or near-death experiences you may have during your life. Aspects to these planets by transit or progression indicate your actual and psychological responses to major changes in your life.

Some people are past the middle of their lives before they lose someone close to them to death. They have not experienced this particular kind of loss and may be poorly prepared to accept the emotional impact of loss. Others have death and near-death experiences much earlier and come to accept transitions in an entirely different way. As you read about the planets that occupy the Eighth House, think of them as visitors who offer the gift of understanding to you or your clients. Each planet in the Eighth is a guide into the underworld, and each will bring you back into the light with renewed energy.

Sun in the Eighth House

You appear fearless as you travel through a life filled with change. You face transitions frequently enough that no one would think you are unfamiliar with death and transformation. Sometimes you overextend yourself, and seem to challenge the Fates by acting recklessly. For you to understand the shaman's message, you must become the shaman. But you don't have to die to gather the necessary wisdom. What needs to die is your desire to use your power only for personal benefit. If you cannot share, then you must at least use your power wisely so that you don't hurt anyone in your personal quest.

Moon in the Eighth House

You are capable of wild emotional swings, and you tend to throw yourself into all of life's activities with all the emotional power you can muster. Other people may tire long before you do. Learn to identify the pace that others can maintain, and slow down sometimes so that they can accompany you on life's journey.

You love the truth, maybe a little too much. You don't have to say every true thing that you know. You can't put the words back in your mouth. The spiritual challenge for you is to feel profoundly, then think deeply, and then speak.

Mercury in the Eighth House

You have two weapons (or tools) for your spiritual journey—the capacity to develop practical skills, and the capacity to speak. If you use your tools to tear apart the work of others and to engage in sarcastic tongue-lashings, then you are operating from a material basis. If you are able to pursue difficult solutions through careful examination of the elements of a problem, and if you speak the truth, wrapping its potent blade with the silk of compassion, then you are well along the spiritual path. You will have extraordinary endurance, whichever way you use your tools.

Venus in the Eighth House

In the end, when everything is done, when you have achieved your goals, you will find them most satisfying if you have behaved well along the way. You attract other people to your point of view easily, and you must remember that they trust you just as much, or more, than you trust them. The key to working with others is to follow a middle path. You need not follow every extreme idea a companion suggests, nor do you need to shy away from all such ideas. Jealousy—the need to keep something just for yourself—is the dark emotion that can be balanced by judicious use of those resources you are willing to share.

Mars in the Eighth House

You are a survivor. On the material or spiritual path, you set goals and attack them consciously. You attract powerful people to yourself, and you enjoy testing your own power. To control others is to lose control of yourself because you are extending yourself beyond your personal boundaries to influence others. To control yourself is to manage your interactions with others through the exercise of compassion. The compassion is first for yourself. Then you can help someone else. It's like they say on airplanes, first put on your own oxygen mask, then help the person next to you.

Jupiter in the Eighth House

You are a materialist, no doubt about it. You are also a spiritual being, on a spiritual path. So while you are gathering those material goods, maintain your own optimism, and encourage someone else to do the same. The path will be rather lonely if you think so much of yourself that no one can live up to your standards. First you must learn to accept your own greater good. What others offer you may not always be what you want, but often it is just what you need. By learning to accept these "gifts" as your spiritual due, you then learn to give to others with both wisdom and love. Progress is swift when this flow is going both ways.

Saturn in the Eighth House

You find that you often take responsibility for other people in some way. You are intelligent, serious, and enjoy problem-solving, even when the problems are very difficult. You also like to drink deeply from the metaphysical well, and you can benefit from meditation practice that allows thinking to be supplemented by intuitive insights. You are likely to experience a spiritual rebirth at least once in your lifetime. This can come after a lot of hard work, or it can come after you have helped others get through their difficulties.

Uranus in the Eighth House

You tend to struggle along the spiritual path, but then you may struggle with a lot of your interactions with other people. Your forceful personality places you "on the edge" frequently, and you become so accustomed to this that you are not happy when things are going too smoothly. You can become a bit reckless, and need to pay close attention to where you are going. Spiritually you are attuned to the future through your intuition. You may see into the next day or next week, and you may be able to discern patterns that extend into the next lifetime. You have senses that reach out like feelers into the current of time. Often you know when major changes will occur for you or for people close to you. Sometimes the only thing you can do with this knowledge is to relax into the changes.

Neptune in the Eighth House

You may have spiritual gifts that you never really had to develop—you just have them. For example, you may be able to see auras around people and objects, and you may be able to read a person's health or emotional state. Whatever your extrasensory gifts, you can use them to help others, and to understand your own spiritual direction more clearly. For example, you can decide not to associate with individuals whose auras seem ugly to you, and you can find ways to cleanse your own aura so that your perceptions are sharper.

Pluto in the Eighth House

How appropriate that Pluto, mythological ruler of the underworld, should be the planetary ruler of the Eighth House of death and transformation. The literature of this planet's namesake is filled with the symbolism of death and rebirth. When Demeter's daughter Kore (Persephone) descended into Hades, Demeter grieved and neglected her worldly duties, causing ceaseless winter. In order to avoid disaster, Zeus decreed that her daughter could return for part of each year. Kali, a Hindu goddess, fought an army of demons and finally defeated them by drinking the blood of her enemy. Yet she is also the source of energy that allows Shiva to exert his power. Inanna, a Sumerian goddess, descended through seven gates into the underworld, leaving behind one symbol of royalty at each gate. She was kept in the underworld for three days by her evil sister, but eventually ascended back into the light to take up her duties again.

It would seem that Pluto, or Hades, attracts the living, but cannot keep a living person in the underworld for long. We are attracted to one way of doing things, but we can't make things stay the same either. As we travel the spiritual path, we find that each ending is the source of a new beginning, and we often benefit from even the most disastrous and traumatic events. By descending into the world of darkness and pain, we borrow a bit of Pluto's power. Then we continue on, stronger and more courageous.

Aspects to the Eighth House Ruler and to Planets in the Eighth House

Aspects show the interplay of transformation in your life. They show which people are involved, and they indicate the quality of the interactions that are most likely to lead to change. Aspects involving the Eighth House are often present for surgery (a change in the physical body), death (the end of a relationship), and all kinds of changes in the flow of material things to and away from you. It is rarely helpful to try to predict death, your own or another person's, as each of us has our own way of approaching that transition. Some people can go through tremendous illnesses or injuries and come out fine, while others succumb to lesser difficulties.

However, it is helpful to observe aspects in the birth chart to see what your natural defenses may be, and what you can expect where other people are concerned. Think of the aspects to the ruler and planets in the Eighth as a résumé of energies that are available to you when your spiritual path transforms you. Each aspect can be seen as a skill you develop for the future spiritual benefit of yourself and others.

Case Study: Elisabeth Kübler-Ross

Elisabeth Kübler-Ross is well known for her research into the psychology of death and dying. Perhaps as a result of her own experience with severe illness as a child, she decided to spend her career helping the dying and their family members accept the process as a natural part of life. She identified five steps in the grieving process: denial, anger, bargaining, grieving, and acceptance. While her work focused on the death process, her method can be applied to all major transformations in life, and you may find that you go through the same steps whenever you are faced with a loss of any kind.

With Saturn in the Eighth House, it is no surprise that Kübler-Ross would be so interested in grief processes. This placement focused her thinking on the profound metaphysical problem of the birth and death cycle, and its impact on individual lives. Saturn trines both the Sun (life) and Pluto (death) in her chart. The square to Neptune connects her to the psychic and psychological nature of major transitions, and the semisextile to the Midheaven indicates her own path to self-awareness.

Pluto is in the Fifth House with the Sun, indicating that her creative processes are closely linked to the life-death process. Pluto squares Mars in the First, reflecting her tireless energy in pursuit of her career goals. The Pluto trine to the Ascendant indicates the power of her personality—she has had a major impact on the psychology of death and dying worldwide. The semisextile to Mercury in the Sixth suggests to me that she may have had a bit of an uphill struggle to articulate her findings to her medical peers.

When your spiritual path provides you with transformation as a spiritual teacher, you may want to review the five steps of the grieving process, as they apply in many life situations. All change involves the inherent loss of something in exchange for something new. Even the most positive changes in our lives can cause us to review our decisions, doubt our direction, and try to hold on to the past.

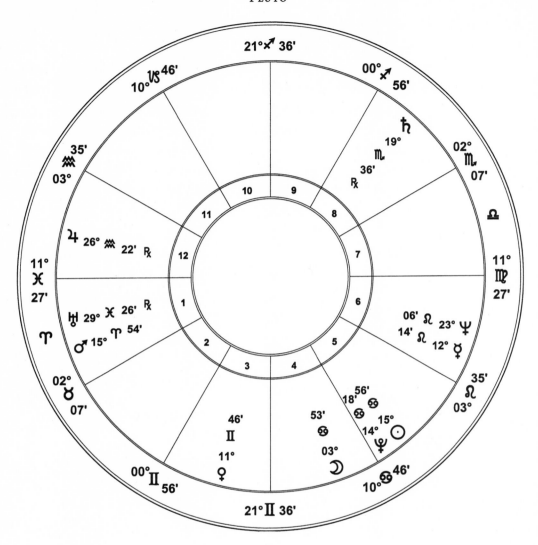

ELISABETH KÜBLER-ROSS
July 8, 1926 / Zurich, Switzerland / 10:45:00 P.M. CET
8E32'00" 47N23'00"

CHAPTER 7

URANUS
Intuition

The planet Uranus indicates by its house placement, sign placement, and aspects the nature of your intuition. Just what is intuition? Intuition is several things:

1. It is the ability to use a capacity of the mind, other than logical thinking, to arrive at a conclusion.

2. According to Carl G. Jung, intuition is one of the four principal ways of apprehending the world. By his definition, intuition is the capacity to consider the future, based on the present.

3. In the Buddhist tradition, intuition is a mental ability, equal to intellect, that can provide insight without relying only on facts to come to a conclusion.

4. In mathematics, intuition is the capacity to "guess" the answer to a problem without pursuing all the mathematical steps to their logical conclusion.

5. Webster defines intuition as "the immediate apprehension or cognition; the power or faculty of attaining to direct knowledge or cognition without evident rational thought and inference; quick and ready insight."

6. Intuition is more than an inner voice. Intuition is a different way to understand the world. It can work with intellect, and you can develop and use it
   consciously.

7. Intuition often arises in the course of meditation. Whatever kind of meditation you practice, it involves calming the conscious mind, and stilling the constant chatter that fills every moment. When the mind is quiet, then intuition
   can arise. Once trained, you can access intuition by slowing your waking mind
   and entering the calm space you have cultivated.

The sign Uranus occupies is the same for all individuals in your age group. Uranus occupies each sign for approximately seven years. The house Uranus occupies is determined by the time of day in which you were born. Aspects of Uranus indicate the ways
in which you develop your intuition.

Equilibrium and Ritual

Uranus reflects how we come back into equilibrium when we have strayed into some
kind of imbalance. The more out of balance we become, the more forceful the impulse
from Uranus will seem. It is the suddenness associated with Uranus that reflects the intuitive leap. Intuition does not dawn over time the way intellectual understanding does.
Instead, intuition leaps into awareness as a "done deal."

Uranus in the Elements

Intuition is often associated with the fire element, and reflects the creativity and future-
oriented inspiration of this element well. However, all the elements have the capacity for
intuition. The element Uranus occupies suggests the direction intuition takes most easily,
and thus defines the futuristic trends of entire groups of people. With an eighty-four-year
cycle, Uranus is in each sign for about seven years. It is possible that everyone in your immediate peer group has Uranus in the same sign, and that people about twenty-eight
years older than you have Uranus in the same element.

Uranus in Fire

Much of your inspiration for your work comes from intuitive insight into future applications and results of your efforts. As your confidence in forecasting develops, you gain

the trust of the people around you. You focus your connection to the spiritual realm through attention to potential future results of today's actions. You are inspired to be your best when you can foresee a positive outcome.

Uranus in Earth

Your intuition comes to you in very concrete images. For example, you can see a piece of land and clearly envision a house, a road, or a bridge being built there. You actually see the finished product in your mind's eye, and then take the practical steps to achieve the result you see. You also can find multiple uses of tools, and can usually handle an emergency with whatever materials and tools you have available.

Uranus in Air

Intuition needs to be thought through. You rely on intellect to resolve questions, and you like to back up your intuition with logic. You gather information intuitively, and then confirm it by asking questions or doing some research. You may not be satisfied about the accuracy of your intuition without some direct confirmation.

Uranus in Water

Your intuition flows more smoothly in a calm environment. Ritual preparation is very helpful in cultivating this kind of insight. Contemplative practice also helps, and this includes more than just sitting on a cushion to meditate. You may find that walking, swimming, or other exercise provides a gateway to expanded intuition.

Uranus in the Signs

Uranus in Aries

You are usually a step ahead of everyone else's game, reaching for the next good idea while handing off today's project to someone else to complete. You enjoy the moment of creation, but even more, the moment before.

Uranus in Taurus

You use your intuition to create equilibrium in your environment. People enjoy being around you because you anticipate their every need. Practical planning is your natural direction. Financial activities benefit from your ability to see future paths and outcomes.

Uranus in Gemini

Where intuition is concerned, you need to develop effective ways to communicate the information you know. By sharing, you stimulate greater insight and benefit from whatever you experience. Some little ritual—like thanking your Source—also helps the flow.

Uranus in Cancer

You are able to perceive the emotional and astral flows of energy, and you often can determine which current to follow before the decisive moment. You touch into energy patterns just enough to gain a sense of direction.

Uranus in Leo

Any leadership role you undertake benefits from your ability to foresee difficult stretches and plan how to manage them. You also have a talent for making your peers or employees feel that they have come up with the ideas themselves.

Uranus in Virgo

You need to apply intuition to your work in a methodical way. Given the future solution you perceive, you have to find the tools you need, even when they are designed for other tasks.

Uranus in Libra

You are often able to perceive the end result of a line of thought or action well ahead of time. Your life has an orderly quality that results from advance information—intuition.

Uranus in Scorpio

You are able to see outcomes, and you may even have the appropriate emotional responses ahead of time. You are well equipped to handle crises because of this advance emotional warning. You are able to call on all of your experience to manage an emergency situation, including awareness of the feelings of other people involved in the crisis.

Uranus in Sagittarius

You are far-seeing, both in terms of distance and time. You like to follow the creative edge in your studies or work, reaching for the next new development with one hand while managing today's business with the other. You may find that you are able to teach others how to access their intuition.

Uranus in Capricorn

Your intuition focuses on how things work, but also on how things will work out in the future. The practical value of intuition in your work may be proven again and again, giving you an edge over the competition.

Uranus in Aquarius

You are comfortable with intuitive information. You listen to your own and also pay attention to insights from people close to you. You can often discern when people are acting on pure hunches, even though they speak of concrete evidence.

Uranus in Pisces

Your empathetic side can see into future feelings, both for yourself and for others. You can master the feelings by sharing what you are sensing. You are often prepared in advance for difficult moments in your life.

Uranus in the Houses

Uranus in the First House

Intuition is first perceived as a natural physical function. In fact, you may be surprised to discover that other people don't share your intuitive capacity. You are able to foresee events and the feelings they will engender in you and the people around you.

Uranus in the Second House

You begin by feeling something—perhaps an itchy feeling—when you come in contact with objects that are psychically charged. You sense the energy infused in them. You can develop the ability to "read" the messages you receive through your senses.

Uranus in the Third House

Your intuition arises through contact with your siblings and peer group. At first it seems that communication occurs through sounds or visual signals. Later it is difficult or impossible for outsiders to detect any communication, but you understand one another even when separated by great distance.

Uranus in the Fourth House

You learn about intuition from family and household members. The ebb and flow of your intuitive sense may be hard to understand at first, but later you learn to wait for it patiently. Your household may include people who are outrageous or just plain crazy. You learn a lot from these people about how to adhere to your own core beliefs.

Uranus in the Fifth House

You begin by noticing that you have thoughts about things that may happen in the future, only to have your thoughts comes true. You can develop the ability to create slightly different outcomes, until eventually you may be able to divert negative events or at least modify the negativity through your own mental effort.

Uranus in the Sixth House

Your intuition works a lot better for other people than it does for you. As you solve problems for others, you will at least reap the benefit of knowing that you are doing good work for them. Find another person to be your intuitive beacon.

Uranus in the Seventh House

Your business or romantic partners stimulate your intuition. Alone, you might ignore this information, but together with a partner you maximize your opportunities for whatever is important to the partnership.

Uranus in the Eighth House

Have you received messages concerning the death of someone before or at the exact moment the death occurred? Have you received direct, clear messages or visitations from someone who has passed on? Even if neither of these has happened, you are specially attuned to the transitions from one phase of life to another, and experience them before the actual event.

Uranus in the Ninth House

Your insight into your studies is especially keen. You know the answers and sometimes have to backtrack to fill in the blanks in problem-solving in order to prove your logic. This intuitive insight can guide you directly to solutions that other people miss.

Uranus in the Tenth House

You often see a clear path out of a problem situation. It's like you "beam" yourself to another location or time, where the difficulty can be resolved. You are quick-thinking in the most difficult situations.

Uranus in the Eleventh House

You are able to discern the movements of groups and you can sometimes perceive the best path through a difficult spot by following energy patterns into the future. Because of your sensitivity, you may avoid large group events, or at least carefully choose the ones you attend.

Uranus in the Twelfth House

Your insight into your past—even past lives—is sometimes very intense. What is more interesting is your unique ability to see into the future, thus reducing any doubts you may have about your current life.

Aspects of Uranus

Aspects involving Uranus pinpoint several possibilities:

1. Areas where conscious attention to ritual can be helpful.

2. The possibilities for conscious focusing of personal energy.

3. Areas where you may experience abrupt changes in your life.

4. Areas where intuition is most likely to develop.

Transiting Uranus is one of the most consistent timers of events. Perhaps this is because the plane of its orbit is very close to that of the Earth. Whatever the reason, as Uranus approaches the exact transiting aspect, events are often sudden, unexpected, and bring major changes. One of my astrology teachers said that if you can think of 100 possible outcomes of a Uranus transit, the one that happens will be number 101. Thus, even though Uranus indicates the focus of intuition—your ability to read into the future—it paradoxically brings totally unforeseen events into your life as well.

CHAPTER 8

SATURN
Karma and Reincarnation

Perhaps no single principle of Asian religions has fascinated us more than karma and its link to reincarnation. It is evident every day that our actions bring reactions in the form of feedback, both constructive and not so constructive. However, much of the everyday feedback comes from individuals who are no more clear about their spiritual values than we are. So what should you take seriously? How does karma work in your life? Will it be delayed until the next incarnation, or do you experience it in the here and now?

You do not have to believe in either karma or reincarnation to make progress along your spiritual path. However, astrology can offer some insight into what factors in the past are influencing you today. The following are suggestions concerning past influences. You can think of them as relating to recent events, to family and childhood experience, to past lives, or all three.

Saturn provides information about karma and dharma. Karma refers to the cause-and-effect relationship between what we do and the results we get. Dharma is the path itself—the work. Most astrologers would say that Saturn is the lord of karma. I prefer to think that Saturn governs dharma. Saturn reflects the possibilities of intelligent activity in the chart.

Some of the best qualities reflected by Saturn are moderation, patience, discipline, and the capacity to learn from experience. Saturn mirrors the structure of whatever you are working with, and this planet also provides a mirror in which you can see yourself. I have found that considering structure is the most helpful way to work with Saturn. Structure is a continuum that reaches from utterly unworkable to sublimely effective action, with all the possible increments of intelligent activity.

Th element Saturn occupies reveals the mental strategy that is most easily available for examining structure in all areas of your life. The element reveals "how" you tend to see things, and Saturn reflects "what" you see. For example, Saturn can represent the structure of how you deal with material things. The range includes acquisitiveness—the capacity for obtaining things. This ability can look like thriftiness—you tend to manage what you have conservatively—or it can look like miserliness—you never let go of anything, no matter what. Saturn's element reflects the mental process you bring to the question of acquiring things.

Saturn in the Elements

Saturn in Fire

Intelligent activity in your life is inspired by your vision. You live in the moment, and you place yourself there in three ways:

1. You welcome the opportunity to make wise decisions. Because of this you dislike being forced to make decisions without thinking things through carefully.

2. You are generally able to look at your past and accept it as just that—the past. Yet you consider the lessons you have learned and apply them to your present life.

3. You use your intuition to prepare for the future. You are often able to forecast future events accurately, even though it seems unlikely that you would know what is going to happen.

Saturn in Earth

Intelligent activity is guided by practical considerations. Your perception of things through sight, touch, and other ordinary senses is your first and strongest avenue to working with the world.

1. You are able to root out the facts by studying history. This uncanny ability may disregard the ephemeral trends of a period and focus instead on the details of the material situation of the time.

2. You are able to mobilize a massive quantity of data, and to organize it to suit your purposes. You sift through data to find the gems that point directly to the conclusion you want to support. Sometimes you have to discover the way to make your conclusions more meaningful to others who are less adept.

3. You use information to guide your intelligence where future plans and goals are concerned. You rarely make long-term decisions based on emotion. It's not that you don't have any feelings, because you do. It's that you know feelings change far more easily than the material foundation on which they rest.

Saturn in Air

You exemplify the best of the thinking process when you are positioning yourself for effective action. You are able to pursue intelligent activity in any area of life where logical thinking prevails over emotions.

1. You are willing to entertain the concept of past lives, but you seldom get caught up in the emotions associated with the past. You examine past events logically and consider how they impact your present decisions, and you learn not to dwell on things that cannot be changed.

2. You make decisions that are generally considered to be wise by your peers. They may approach you with passionate arguments, strange futuristic plans, or even hard-edged "facts," but you apply your logic equally to each of these, and make decisions that everyone can live with.

3. In preparing for the future, you are able to formulate a plan and project it into the future mentally, observing how the turnings of each part of the plan affect other systems. Your plans become more effective when you seek the counsel of individuals who use each of the four strategies in their planning, as you can make use of their thinking style within your logical approach.

Saturn in Water

Intelligent activity, for you, is inspired by the feeling component of your mind. You can make a plan using any of the mental strategies, but you evaluate and judge its efficacy through the feeling function.

1. In looking back on your own past, into past lives, or even ancient human history, you judge people's actions by the results they achieved, and you also consider whether those results were worth the effort. Even if the outcome was what people wanted and needed, you evaluate the effectiveness of the action.

2. You are able to learn from the past and to exercise good judgment in almost everything you do. You may tend toward caution in your planning, and you gather information at every step of the process. Because of sensitive positioning, you are able to make adjustments to suit the needs of the moment.

3. You like to have the time to project your plan into the future to think through the possible outcomes. When you feel rushed into implementing a plan, you may be reluctant if you cannot see a positive outcome. For this reason, it may be difficult to have faith in someone else's plan.

Saturn in the Signs

How you work is a metaphor for how you progress on the path of spiritual development. Saturn serves as a teacher on several levels:

1. First, you learn from your day-to-day encounters, including both failures and successes.

2. Second, Saturn may be the reflection of your attempt to grapple with lessons brought with you from prior lifetimes.

3. Third, Saturn provides the testing ground for beliefs and values that can carry you forward in your spiritual journey.

The goal is perfection. Remembering this allows you to make mistakes, as you have not reached the goal—you are still learning and growing.

Saturn in Aries

The spiritual path will transmute your material ambition into the higher aspiration to use intelligent activity in service to humanity. Instead of ruling, you aspire to be the facilitator of each person's individual progress.

Saturn in Taurus

What can be stubborn insistence on getting your own way in your work and relationships can become the perseverance that is needed to work out your karmic attachments, and to pursue your personal dharma. Slow, steady advancement is preferred.

Saturn in Gemini

The thoroughness of your logical mind is the cornerstone of all progress. The very fact that you are not the most adaptable person is the reason you are so skilled in tackling complex problems, as you don't let go until you have reached a satisfying conclusion.

Saturn in Cancer

Your karmic progress depends not only on how you become aware of and deal with karmic issues. Effective action also includes nurturing yourself and others skillfully. Study both methods and values.

Saturn in Leo

People experience you as being shy—you don't jump right into social situations, but sit back to see which way the energy is moving. You have one eye on the outcome of each situation, and are usually able to foresee difficulties and head them off.

Saturn in Virgo

You can be a nag with your attention to details. Yet you feel the responsibility to tie up loose ends so that they don't trip you up later. Other people may misunderstand your actions and see you as critical or obsessive.

Saturn in Libra

You are the quintessential partner—loyal, hard working, and steadfast. Your sense of duty keeps you in relationships well past the point where other people would have thrown in the towel. You are initially reluctant to engage in serious romantic or business partnerships because you know you won't be able to disengage easily.

Saturn in Scorpio

Your intense focus on the metaphysical realm can distract you from the demands of physical relationships. Sexual energy can be inhibited unless you can see that the path to ecstasy includes all levels of consciousness. You see the spiritual value in all life, and understand birth and death as necessary transitions.

Saturn in Sagittarius

Your sense of justice can be harsh if you focus only on the words of human and spiritual laws, and not on the intention. Doubt may arise when you have not spent enough time in meditation and reflection. Spiritual and other desires may take you far from your birthplace.

Saturn in Capricorn

You are industrious in every activity you undertake. You expect effective action from yourself and from others and can be a harsh or willful manager. Through experience you move from an egocentric attitude to self-awareness. Then you advance much more quickly, both economically and spiritually.

Saturn in Aquarius

Social situations bring out the best in you. You are effective in groups and are able to encourage harmonious relationships among others. Your mental approach to planning needs the solid foundation these other people can provide through their diverse viewpoints.

Saturn in Pisces

You are generally retiring, and may even decide on a life of renunciation—at least for a time. Your mystical tendencies are well suited to the contemplative life, and you wish to avoid any unnecessary conflict. You are your own best source of recognition, as you are the best person to evaluate the effectiveness of your decisions and actions.

Saturn in the Houses

There is a particular direction in which your intelligent activity will most likely move. It is where you position yourself and represents your strongest capacities as a human being.

Saturn in the First House

Your lessons come from your sense of personal responsibility. You are ambitious in terms of career and material things, and your ambition extends to your spiritual life as well. As you transcend selfish ambitions, you engage instead in the pursuit of higher spiritual aspirations, which are firmly grounded in your ability to learn from all your experiences.

Saturn in the Second House

Your most significant karmic lesson involves self-esteem and self-worth. Resolve responsibilities and pain from the past. Then you become a vehicle for conscious intelligent action—you recognize the karma your actions may create.

Saturn in the Third House

Your teacher is a stern disciplinarian. Perfection is what you seek, yet you may experience sorrow, disappointment, and limitation along the path. You will be required to give up old habits and thought patterns in order to form more adaptable, purer structures for your emerging spirituality. All this is designed to teach you self-discipline first, and compassion later.

Saturn in the Fourth House

In your youth you learned from your elders and listened carefully to their ideas and beliefs. Now you find you are able to share key principles and values with your own students or the younger generation of your family.

Saturn in the Fifth House

You are very reliable and intensely loyal, and expect the same from other people. Romantic love may be hampered by a sense of caution—or even shyness—that keeps you from being open to physical expression. You are able to perceive the structure of creative potential in all areas of your life, and find spiritual meaning in creative projects.

Saturn in the Sixth House

You are exacting in your work, seeking perfection that will necessarily elude you some of the time. On the spiritual level you are compassionate toward others, and you learn to be compassionate toward yourself. Your keen observation skills provide the information you need to make decisions.

Saturn in the Seventh House

You bring loyalty to any partnership, romantic or otherwise. Your conscientious behavior helps you reap the greatest spiritual value from each serious contact you make, as you seldom run away from responsibilities, once you have accepted them. You learn not to jump into relationships too quickly, as you plan to stay for the long haul.

Saturn in the Eighth House

You have a very serious approach to life, as you understand the profound significance of the birth-life-death process. You explore the metaphysical values that underlie each transition in your life, and you are well equipped to help others do the same. You will likely experience a spiritual rebirth in this lifetime.

Saturn in the Ninth House

Events that focus your attention on transcendent values have to do with time, authority, and responsibility. You tend to be harder on yourself than anyone else is because you expect perfection in yourself. When disagreements arise with others, you may take them to heart, worrying about what you could have done differently, even if there was no other possible outcome. Qualities that Saturn helps you develop include patience, compassion, and humility. You know very well that your skills are gifts from a higher source, and you learn to apply them to tasks in your life without feeling spiritual pride in your own actions. As you experience the death of loved ones and the weakening of your own physical powers, you come to understand the cyclical nature of physical life and the immortality of spirit.

Saturn in the Tenth House

Your strong will furthers your career and supports your social position. You believe that steady work serves you well on the material level, and it works well in terms of spirit too. Your tendency to follow a narrow line of thinking provides strong focus, but may cause you to miss the richness of possibilities that surround you. The plus side is that this same focus helps you get right to the heart of the subject at hand.

Saturn in the Eleventh House

Your ideals and creativity align to bring solid results. You are a reliable partner or group member, always striving to keep your end of every agreement. A good practice is to set generous, not excessive goals, and to use your spiritual values as part of the skill set you bring to each project.

Saturn in the Twelfth House

Your karmic history is available for exploration in the quiet moments of privacy we all need. Examine your past behavior, but only for the purpose of seeking more effective action in the future.

CHAPTER 9

JUPITER
Transcendent Values

Behind what you know about yourself—behind all other considerations of spirituality, lie the transcendent values that are most important to you. These are the values you may have spent time trying to discover, to sift from among all the rules you have been taught. They are the reason you have read books, studied with teachers, and privately mulled over the events of your life. They are the fundamental principles that you believe will help you to find fulfillment as a human being. As such they are the potential energy behind your self-awareness, the motivation of your spiritual search, and the principles that you apply to your dharma, or life path.

Guideposts along your path are life experiences that evoke or reveal the qualities of spirit around you and within you. Your subjective purpose in life is to understand heart and mind as one Unity. You gain the ability to replace conflict in your life with transcendent wisdom, and the capacity to express love easily and fluidly. Life's problems become points of interest along the spiritual path, and are no longer obstacles to your development. Spirit then acts through you as both master and servant, and you expand your heart and mind toward a Universal purpose. You remain open to all life, while listening to the inner guidance of your higher values.

Jupiter in the Elements

Jupiter reflects your capacity for generosity, idealism, faith, expansion, and success. Jupiter and the Ninth House indicate how optimism can become a more significant factor in your daily life. On the spiritual plane Jupiter goes far beyond these ordinary functions to delineate the way you organize all your energy and activities—Jupiter reflects how you process sensations, feelings, and thoughts.

Ultimately Jupiter shows how the fusion of heart and mind occurs in your life. The synthesis of love and wisdom is inevitable on the spiritual path. The element and sign placement of Jupiter serve as indications of the primary direction of your search for spiritual values and their application to the problems you face every day. Jupiter also shows one path toward fuller opening of the heart.

Jupiter in Fire

You feel more optimistic and successful when your daily activities incorporate intuition in a meaningful way. Whatever your natural direction, based on your Sun and Moon elements, you can develop intuition as a spiritual guidance mechanism. You may find that you become physically sensitive in the heart area—you may feel heat in the skin on your chest or back, for example. This change in temperature can serve as an intuitive barometer.

When your human energies are spiritually directed, you approach the moment when you are no longer subject to the ordinary limitations of the physical world. Your mind and heart foresee the karmic effects of your actions and you can make intelligent choices. Then you are no longer limited by the wheel of birth and rebirth, and can fully experience the life for which you are intended.

Jupiter in Earth

While Jupiter is your guide to the spiritual life, the path is through actions in the material realm. You function best when your heart and mind join forces in ordinary activities, making the most of each opportunity. Your faith grows in the fertile soil—literally and figuratively. Your optimism flourishes when you are in physical surroundings that emphasize the beauty of life and the spiritual expression in growth, blossoming, and bearing fruit. Spiritually your response is no different—you seek expansion of your mind and heart into arenas of expression that resonate with your higher being.

When your mind and heart are synchronized, you find that the material details of your life flow into a pattern of success, sustaining your faith and providing what you need to help others. Your vision of life focuses on the present moment, even though you understand the karmic flow of events on a profound level. When you are expressing the fusion of heart and mind fully, you radiate warmth, your aura expands, and you possess great dignity, even in stressful moments.

Jupiter in Air

Regardless of your typical mental style, indicated by the element occupied by the Sun, you are more skilled in logical thinking and the skillful use of words than in the use of emotions. You aspire to more perfect expression, both within yourself and in the social realm. Mental and spiritual training benefit you by providing rigorous reasoning skills and by opening your heart to the intuitive information that flows around you.

Even when you have achieved fusion of heart and mind, you find that your mental process and expression focus on intellect and the thinking process. You may come to trust your intuition deeply, but you gain this level of confidence through testing your intuitive knowledge logically and rationally. You understand that the cycle of cause and effect begins on the mental plane, descends through the emotional realm, and manifests in the physical world.

Jupiter in Water

You find it easy to expand your emotional range to encompass other people, large projects, and even global thinking. You naturally want to engage with others because this is one of the principal ways you learn. While you may use intellect skillfully in your daily activities, it is at the emotional heart level that you connect to the planet, to humanity, and to spirit.

It may seem that fusion of heart and mind is easier when Jupiter is in a water sign because we ordinarily experience the values of the heart in an emotional way. However, such fusion is not limited to water signs, nor do water signs limit the possible expression of transcendent values in any way. One advantage to this placement is that a constant flow of spiritual energy is possible. You may benefit from a meditation practice that focuses on the flows of energy through your body, whether it be breath or energy on a higher plane.

Jupiter in the Signs

The sign placement of Jupiter indicates the way you expand your vision to include the whole of your experience, and it reflects the focus of your spiritual aspirations.

Jupiter in Aries

You are capable of leadership in any activity you engage in because of your innate honesty, generosity, and organizational ability. Spiritual growth proceeds more smoothly when you engage in contemplative practice and associate with individuals of high moral and ethical character.

Jupiter in Taurus

You are capable of enjoying life to its fullest on the physical level and you may excel in financial dealings. Spiritual growth can occur in this environment when you employ ethical and moral principles in your decision-making process, and resist being swayed by the argument of the moment.

Jupiter in Gemini

Your versatility makes you the welcome guest at any gathering. You thrive on the many social connections that feed your self-awareness and spiritual bank account. Because you love change, you move forward on the spiritual path with relative ease, as long as you keep your own values in mind.

Jupiter in Cancer

Your strong sense of family and hereditary values guides your work and inspires your emotional life. Contemplative practice should be designed to help you focus on one spiritual target. In this way you develop the capacity to focus in all areas of your life.

Jupiter in Leo

Self-confidence makes you a strong leader, and you gain popularity in direct proportion to your personal ethical input. Contemplative practice that focuses on the inner space of your heart and mind will serve to align your spiritual aspirations with your activities in the world at large.

Jupiter in Virgo

You have strong ethical and moral principles. They may seem to get in the way, sometimes, when you feel compelled to take a stand rather than go with the flow. Limit criticism of others to what is necessary, and practice service and cooperation each day.

Jupiter in Libra

You have a strong sense of justice, and are well able to work for the public good. You may tend to depend on cooperation from others more than you need to. Contemplative practice develops the capacity to depend on your inner resources first.

Jupiter in Scorpio

You are somewhat ruthless in your striving for emotional fulfillment that falls short of your spiritual aspirations. Instead of focusing on physical pleasure, contemplative practice can elevate your material desire to the level of spiritual yearning. Then all activities—even sexual—can provide spiritual ecstasy.

Jupiter in Sagittarius

You seek inner spiritual development in everything you do. Your mind reaches far into the future, and such speculation can become its own problem if you don't ground your intuition in something more practical. Contemplative practice can include walking or working meditation that connects you to the material realm directly.

Jupiter in Capricorn

Your practicality and sense of duty may lead to leadership situations in all areas of your life. Contemplative practice helps clarify the difference between what you expect of yourself, and what you require from others. Worldly duties may or may not be consistent with your spiritual path.

Jupiter in Aquarius

You may confuse social justice with spiritual values. They are not the same. Contemplative practice helps you understand your inner nature, distinguish it from your awareness of other people, and direct your spiritual path according to your personal needs and aspirations.

Jupiter in Pisces

If you have no contemplative guidance system, you can fall prey to moods induced by alcohol and drugs. What works better is a relatively quiet life, or at least finding a quiet space in which you can retreat from the emotional impressions swirling around you. Then the spiritual path can make itself known to you.

The Sign on the Ninth House Cusp

The sign of the zodiac on the cusp of the Ninth House reflects the transcendent themes that are the most important in your life. You will likely find that values specific to other signs also resonate with you, but the first focus will be on the sign on the Ninth House cusp.

Aries on the Ninth House Cusp

The transcendent values with which you work begin with the capacity to exert your personal will in the world—to be what you want to be and do what you want to do. By understanding this value, you can then begin to manifest creatively in both the material and spiritual worlds. You find that sometimes you feel as though you are engaged in a battle of proper expression, and you seek to encourage others in the same direction. All your efforts—to be, to do, and to encourage others—lead to Unity, but you must exert effort in the process. Matter is the vehicle for expression in the physical world, and the soul is your vehicle on the higher plane. Spirit is the third factor you seek to understand.

Taurus on the Ninth House Cusp

The first transcendent value for you to understand is the capacity to express your inner urges on the physical plane. While stubbornness is nobody's idea of transcendent expression, it is the source of your persistent efforts to express yourself. With practice you arrive at the second value—will and intelligence working together. As you identify and pursue your soul's purpose, you find that you are no longer acting out of personal desire, but that an impulse to love others is guiding you. The third value is the use of spiritual will. At this level you will understand the Unity of Mind, and you will be able to move in a spiritual direction, using the persistence you developed on the physical plane, along with intelligence guided by love. The power you will then have truly transcends ordinary physical limits.

Gemini on the Ninth House Cusp

The first value you have to understand is perceived duality in the physical world. Because all perceptions are a function of this perception, you will need to sharpen your powers of observation, and learn to perceive things without judgment. A second value lies in the understanding of change. You have the capacity to understand the processes of change on every level of the mind. As you gain this understanding you come to see the consistency of change within the whole of being. The third value is abstract mental power. You learn the ability to exert your intelligence, free of attachment to the material world, gaining "concrete" knowledge on the spiritual plane. Then you can understand the true causes behind all manifestation.

Cancer on the Ninth House Cusp

The first transcendent value for you is instinctual awareness. Because instinct is often thought to be a primitive function in animals, you may question this value, but it is, nonetheless, a first principle for you. If you cannot depend on your instincts, you have no firm ground from which to proceed. The second value is mass consciousness. As you gain understanding of instincts, you begin to appreciate how they work in group situations. Your relationships to others are both the source of, and the resolution of, personal karma. The third value is devotion. You come to understand how instincts are related to self-preservation and the fulfillment of needs. You also understand the expression of devotion when a crowd of people follow one man or woman, seemingly instinctually. Finally you experience the power of devotion to a spiritual goal, supported by all your instincts and experience.

Leo on the Ninth House Cusp

At first you may not feel that self-consciousness is a particularly transcendent value, but it is the cornerstone for effective action in the world. You must understand yourself as an individual being before you can undertake any steps along the evolutionary path. The second value, physical nature, is a primary aid to self-consciousness. Until you understand yourself as a physical being in the material world, you will only struggle with concepts of Unity. By pursuing self-awareness in the depths of physical, mental, and emotional experience, you can discover a sense of personal unity, and through this means, a sense of universal oneness. If you seek to lead others, you must first gain a clear understanding of your own being and the evolutionary path that you are pursuing.

Virgo on the Ninth House Cusp

The transcendent values you seek to understand are three expressions of the feminine. The first expression is Eve—the search for knowledge in the physical world. This value is expressed on the mental plane. The second value involves taking the quest for knowledge to the emotional plane. The third value is the expression of knowledge on the physical plan through creation. These three values relate to the expression of mind into physical form and creative work in the material world. This involutionary process can be compared to the evolutionary process whereby the receptive mind becomes the expressive agent of the spirit.

Libra on the Ninth House Cusp

The transcendent value you most resonate with is equilibrium. You experience duality in the physical, mental, and spiritual realms, but you seek to maintain balance. You understand duality but are able to rest in a meditative state without engaging in either extreme. A second value is the capacity for judgment. If you can place yourself in a balanced position, then you can exercise judgment that is not complicated by egoistic aims. A third value is desire. Physical and sexual desires have the purpose of fulfilling personal needs as well as transcendent ones. For you, focusing on desire is an effective path to understanding the nature of opposites and the elevation of physical motivations to the level of spiritual aspiration.

Scorpio on the Ninth House Cusp

The first transcendent value you seek to grasp is that the path of discipleship is yours. You are on it and you need to mobilize your whole being to pursue it. The second value lies in understanding that you as an individual and the human race as a whole are at a turning point. Evolutionary processes can either go forward, leaving behind ideas of self-aggrandizement, or they can slip back into the material struggle and remain focused on physical desires. Reorientation, however, does not demand that you give up the material to seek the spiritual. You can take your entire skill set with you on the path. The third value is to develop sensitivity to the larger plan of the universe. As you become more attuned to spiritual potential, you gain the capacity to moderate your own desires and to respond to the spiritual desires of others.

Sagittarius on the Ninth House Cusp

While human emotions may not seem transcendent, understanding them is one of your highest values. This is important for you as an individual, and it is also significant in the way you interact with others. A second value is focused consciousness. Learning to focus is key to proper orientation to your work, whether in the material or spiritual realm. Without focus, your work wanders all over the map, never reaching its destination. A third transcendent principle lies in the perceived duality of physical existence. You find many ways to understand the illusion of duality, and to help others understand it as well. As you become aware of these specific values, you find that your efforts follow as sure a path as that of an arrow shot from a bow, and the power of your path lies in your personality, just as the power of the arrow is inherent in both arrow and bow.

Capricorn on the Ninth House Cusp

The reality of concrete materialization is the first transcendent value you meet. Because you have a firm grip on physical reality, this may not seem transcendent, but it is important to any future tasks. The second value lies in understanding completion. You seek to finish the tasks you begin—for you the outcome is perhaps more important than the means. Appreciation of the means is something you may want to develop. A third value is in the understanding of new or renewed effort. Once you achieve the pinnacle of personal expression on the physical or spiritual plane, you will recognize that yet another goal is in sight, and you reorient your efforts to that end. What is perceived as a real struggle or strain may become a more friendly path, both for you and for those around you.

Aquarius on the Ninth House Cusp

Your primary transcendent focus is on group consciousness. This focus is a most significant factor in your personal development, as it is the inspiration for selflessness. A second transcendent value is your lower mental nature. Intellectual development is key to your spiritual progress. Note that group consciousness is primary, and that personal intellect serves a supporting role. A third value is the truth of Unity or Universal Mind. It is through the intuitive understanding of the oneness of all existence that you are able to mobilize your intellect in the service of group consciousness. As these values become the motivation for your conscious actions, you will find that your spirit flows like water from an endless source, enriching the lives of others as you move toward personal liberation.

Pisces on the Ninth House Cusp

The first transcendent value you seek to understand is slavery. You may seek to understand the physical attachments you have to others and to ideas as slavery, whether it is imposed on you or you impose it on yourself. The second value is detachment. As you come to understand the material or mental restrictions you experience, you can become more detached, viewing them from a less emotional perspective. The third value is death—death to the bonds that keep you from freely expressing your spirit, and also death as a material and spiritual doorway into a new experience. When these values are understood, you find that service to others is no longer a trial, but instead a conscious expression of your will on several levels of consciousness.

Jupiter in the Houses

Jupiter's position in the houses indicates the area of your life where your transcendent values are revealed. We often find that we look in all the wrong places for what we need. Consider the house placement of your Ninth House ruler. This area of your life may indeed provide the grist for your spiritual mill. This is especially true if there are no planets in the Ninth House to focus your values clearly.

Jupiter in the First House

The root of your transcendent values lies within your personality and your childhood experience. It is therefore important for you to consider your life experience as a valuable spiritual asset, not to be discarded lightly when you hear about a different religion, or when you fall in love with the teachings of a particular individual. Whatever you pursue, it needs to mesh with your personal experience.

Jupiter in the Second House

Your transcendent values grow out of an understanding of the material basis of your life, and from your self-esteem. Until you have established yourself as a valuable being, and until you value your own life, you will find that transcendent values elude you. It is your ability to persevere through great difficulty that eventually moves you forward on the path. As you move forward, you are able to consolidate your life experiences into a package of skills that aid your spiritual growth every bit as much as they aid your physical and emotional well-being.

Jupiter in the Third House

The most important influence on your transcendent values is your interaction with others. Thus it is imperative that you cultivate an environment filled with people who encourage your developmental process. Seek out people who offer positive experiences. Avoid people who seem to drag you down to the lowest levels of human expression. This may occasionally mean ending relationships, changing jobs, or moving to a new location as you seek to surround yourself with what you need. Eventually you are able to transcend the less constructive influences in your environment, and then you can work to change the level of consciousness directly.

Jupiter in the Fourth House

The deepest, richest source of transcendent values lies within your family and home experience. You may find this difficult to understand at first, particularly if your childhood family situation was not totally positive. However, beneath any negativity there resides a foundation of beliefs that provides a starting point for your spiritual search. Hereditary values are a powerful ground on which to build personal beliefs. The key is to identify and retain what suits your quest, and set aside what does not work. You are deeply influenced by philosophy. You study the past and discuss it with family members in order to clarify your own values.

Jupiter in the Fifth House

The multiple expressions of your creative drive form the transcendent process. The sexual impulse can be a strong focus for you, as physical ecstasy provides its moment of spiritual transcendence. Any creative activity you engage in draws on spiritual energy and reveals it at the same time. Each successful effort builds your confidence so that you can reach greater heights. Define or redefine your work and play as creative activities, and look for the spiritual spark within each of them.

Jupiter in the Sixth House

Karma yoga may be your path to transcendent values. Your work is very important to you. You tend to pursue all your life's activities with a certain diligence and attention. Your spiritual path is no different. It is imperative that your work environment be conducive to your spiritual development. No amount of financial remuneration can make up for a job that oppresses you and prevents you from expressing your values in a positive manner. By the same token, a suitable work environment—the right location and the right people—can make the most mundane of tasks into a spiritual process.

Jupiter in the Seventh House

Your spirit thrives in communion with other people. This can involve a romantic life partner, a business partnership, or other cooperative efforts. Communes are designed around the concept of shared work, play, and spiritual pursuits, to draw out the spirit. Your choices of partners, then, form the basis of trust that leads you to understand your transcendent values. And remember, you do not have to share each and every value of your partner in order for both of you to grow. What you share is the desire to support and learn from each other.

Jupiter in the Eighth House

Birth and death are your most powerful spiritual teachers. In the living events of your life you find both struggle and attainment. You face losses on a daily basis and you can use these experiences to understand your relationship with spirit. You also experience the birth of new ideas and feelings all the time. As you develop an understanding of the rhythm of life and death, you approach an understanding of transcendence in your life.

Jupiter in the Ninth House

You will find your values within your studies. It is essential that you develop a formal approach to learning. This does not have to be a college degree program. It can involve reading, attending workshops and seminars on subjects of interest to you, or traveling to sites where spiritual energy is focused. You can choose which traditions to pursue, and you may be drawn to a philosophy or religion very different from what you were taught as a child. You are the perennial student, always willing to expand your sphere of knowledge.

Jupiter in the Tenth House

Spiritual goals are part and parcel of your career path. A career without these values is no career in your mind. You generally take a serious attitude toward life. You feel you don't have the time to waste on anything that does not move you toward both your material and spiritual goals. It is important, whatever your career, to identify the path within that field that allows you to do your spiritual work. You are called to your work, and you will want to profess the best of that work, so that at the end of your life you can feel you have managed well on every level of expression.

Jupiter in the Eleventh House

Circumstances lead you to spiritual transcendence. In one sense you may feel that no matter what you do, you will eventually find what you are seeking. In another sense, however, you influence your course by right thought. Often what you think is precisely what you get. In the cases where this is not so true, you can examine your thoughts, compare them with the apparent results, and modify your desires for the future. You have a knack for taking action at the right moment.

Jupiter in the Twelfth House

Traditionally you would have taken contemplative vows and sought the seclusion of monastic life. In that setting you would have had daily tasks to perform, but you would also have had many hours to focus on spirit. In the modern world you may not have this luxury of time, so you need to address your spiritual needs carefully and create a suitable space for your meditation or other spiritual pursuits. Because you are open and receptive, you may want to structure your private space so that it draws in the highest spiritual energy possible. Traditional religious or ethnic objects may help you maintain an environment conducive to contemplation.

Planets in the Ninth House

Planets in the Ninth House indicate strong influences that shape your transcendent values. These influences can be individuals who have had a significant impact on your formulation of values throughout your life. They could be teachers, religious figures, or members of the legal system who have played roles in your life. They can also indicate events that have intervened to push you in certain directions. Your experiences in higher education, travel, or church activities are examples of events that play a part in the development of transcendent values. Finally, they represent those conditions that cause you to address your values in new ways. For example, a Ninth House conjunction might indicate an educational career filled with turmoil. Other aspects to Ninth House planets might indicate your capacity to endure a long-distance move.

Aspects to the Ninth House Ruler and to Planets in the Ninth House

The closest aspect to Jupiter indicates the kinds of people and activities that support your spiritual growth, and the nature of that support. This aspect often indicates an early influence in your life that set the tone for your religious or ethical beliefs, and can define the pattern and scope of your spiritual life.

Case Study: Muhammad Ali

Jupiter in Gemini in the Tenth House is a solid indication of Ali's glib poetry and his insistence on his own greatness throughout his boxing career. We could be lulled into thinking that this individual is a superficial thinker with nothing on his mind but the next conquest in the ring. But during and after his boxing career, Ali has pursued his religious beliefs. His page on the National Geographic website includes an essay in which he states, "My religion teaches me that God wants us to love one another. And I believe that love, not hate, is at the heart of God's master plan" (www.nationalgeographic. com-faces/ali/main.html).

CHAPTER 10

THE MIDHEAVEN
Developing Self-Awareness

How can you use your self-awareness to access intuition, a presumably involuntary, less conscious capacity? To take the direct, conscious path is challenging at best. This method only works if you can consciously enter the unconscious territory, and by definition, that territory is unconscious because you cannot access it directly. You can rarely dive in intentionally.

You can wait for intuition to arise naturally without doing anything. The action is like an artesian spring, where water is pushed up from deep under the ground because of pressure. This method allows you to get intuitive information, but only on a hit or miss basis. You have little control over the process. However, by paying attention to what intuitive messages come, this approach operates more freely.

You can practice meditation. This method establishes a sacred space in which intuition can be encouraged. This method has the advantage of being under conscious control. It is also something you can do when and where you choose. It is fairly easy to learn and requires no particular physical or mental skills, except the ability to focus the mind.

Awareness, Intellect, and Insight

Where intuition is concerned, awareness means knowledge gathered through your own observation. It is firsthand information. It is gathered through thought and the senses, but is neither of these. It involves the process of recognition. It demands that you see things as they are. Some people call this conscious awareness.

Intellect is the capacity for rational thought. It generally involves both inductive and deductive reasoning processes. Insight is a combination of intellect and intuition, in which all avenues to awareness are incorporated.

Meditation

You do not need to engage in a complicated process to begin meditation. In fact, you probably have engaged in all the activities included here in the process. Begin by sitting cross-legged on a cushion or sitting comfortably in a chair with your feet on the floor. Sit with your back straight to facilitate the breathing process. Rest your hands on your thighs. You can close your eyes, but it is often helpful to keep them open, gazing ahead and downward without particular focus. Then simply pay attention to your breath. Follow it out, be aware of the natural in-breath, and follow it out again.

When your mind is distracted, identify the distraction as thinking and return to the breath. At first you will find that most of your time is spent in these distracting thoughts. Don't judge them, just label them and return to the breath. The process is designed to train you to focus on one thing. The thoughts that arise are your internal resistance to the process of becoming focused.

Meditation practice will help you develop skills that both allow intuition to arise and allow you to identify it. First you learn to narrow the focus of your mind. Second, you learn to maintain awareness of whatever object is within that focus, and you learn to do this without judging. You become aware of the focus itself, and of the particular quality of focused attention. In doing this, you bring your whole being, both your conscious mental process, emotions, and physical skills, and your unconscious instincts and desires, into the present situation. Thus you have both available to you at the same time. The unconditional, nonjudgmental quality of meditation is what allows intuition to become conscious.

As mentioned above, no part of the meditation process is really new. You know how to sit, you know how to breathe, and you know how to focus. Meditation simply helps develop the skill of focusing. By focusing on one thing to the exclusion of thoughts, you allow a gap to appear in the mind. Such a gap is needed in order for insight (intuition) to arise. And in fact no part of the outcome is new. You already have experienced the skills described here. The value of meditation is that you will be able to call on these skills more readily, and you will be able to maintain focus more steadily.

In addition to the above approach to meditation, you have specific avenues, or points of focus, to aid you in the practice. The sign on the Midheaven indicates an area of the subconscious that you can access through meditation, thereby identifying spiritual keys to your development. By going within, you find the higher values most suited to your own path.

The Midheaven in the Signs

The Midheaven in Aries

Beneath a subconscious desire to have significant interpersonal relationships, you find the capacity to understand many different areas of study. You soak up information easily, both through individual study and group cooperative efforts. Of the masses of data presented to you, you naturally categorize and store facts for future use. It is important not to confuse this kind of knowledge with practical experience, which you can develop only through contact with others.

You seek the perfection of harmony in all your dealings, and the information most available to you centers on balance and harmony in relationships. This tendency extends to how you understand yourself as well. You gather information that helps you achieve harmonious communication with your inner self, your spiritual being, and your unconscious mind. Dreams reflect the degree of balance you have achieved, and also offer more concrete information about the less defined realms of the mind.

The Midheaven in Taurus

Your unconscious relationship to power probably began in childhood. Depending on how your parents or other authority figures exercised their power, you have learned patterns of behavior and methods for getting your own way. It is important to become very conscious of these patterns, as they can be valuable conscious resources or treacherous swamps of ineffective unconscious behavior.

You have a deeply rooted capacity for healing yourself and others. When you are in tune with this ability, you are able to accomplish transformations in the emotional systems that surround you, thus transforming the effectiveness of your associates and family. Through understanding your personal values and strengths, you can learn to exercise your own power fairly and judiciously, while retaining the capacity to exert force on every level when that is needed.

The Midheaven in Gemini

Beneath the subconscious desire to hibernate in your own home, you discover the profound aspiration to develop a spiritual life. While your family may have focused on learning, travel, and formal religion, you are more interested in a mystical understanding of yourself in the phenomenal world. You do this through the cultivation of wisdom first, and then merge that wisdom with the love principle. Early in life you come to understand the fundamental dualism of the body/mind, and you grow out of a desire to simply satisfy the body. As an adult you transcend this duality and become more and more aware of the spiritual dualism that pervades your being. You come to see that the body is a vehicle—a servant—for spirit, and as such, the body must be carefully tended, but it no longer is the sole arbiter of comfort.

Keep in mind that your core beliefs will not become radically different. Rather, there is a building process you experience. Because of your unconscious impulse to bring about a fusion of heart and mind, casting off old beliefs is not an effective approach. The melding of the old and new results in less influence from the old, as it is moderated by the spiritual insight you gain throughout your life. It is through synthesis of your experience that you approach your spiritual goals, and it is through this kind of understanding that you can act wisely and compassionately to help others.

The Midheaven in Cancer

Beneath the subconscious desire to be the authority figure in your own life, you find you seek intelligent activity. Not one to be satisfied with methods you learn from others, you seek to formulate your own procedures, based on factual knowledge, personal experience, and instruction or training from established sources. In the process of developing better processes, you may appear dictatorial, limiting the activities of others or restricting them to what you approve of. True intelligent activity will come to allow the creative problem solving of others to play a part, with you acting more as a guidance system.

Your understanding of how to direct activity effectively helps get you past any rigid controlling behaviors. Each experience is assimilated into your matrix of resources, expanding your potential to be more effective in the future. You learn to engage in more effective action and thus become a valuable asset within your family, work, and social spheres, as you can be depended on to find more satisfactory solutions for personal and interpersonal problems.

The Midheaven in Leo

Beneath the subconscious desire to formalize all interactions in your life into patterns, you find the rich capacity to create rituals that satisfy deep personal and social needs. You learn first from family, and later from teachers, friends, employers, and others, about the subtle relationships and movement that reflect ritual response. You see the differences between individual energy and group energy, and learn to modify your own behavior to suit different situations. This goes beyond simply wearing the "right" clothes and exhibiting the "right" manners. It becomes an intuitive awareness of proper action and knowledge of future results of your present actions.

You move from a simple practitioner of good manners to a capable manager of social interactions. You recognize the craving people have for proper ritual in the intense interest in the past. Historically, societies wove ritual patterns into all-important interactions with people, animals, gods, and the earth. You are able to identify the ritual processes that are missing from certain situations and incorporate them into your own behavior, thus filling a deeply felt gap and healing situations in the process.

The Midheaven in Virgo

You have a deeply rooted psychic capacity. You can, if you open yourself to the world around you, feel the emotional emanations of people, animals, and objects. Even if you aren't conscious of this ability, you use it to steer a course of safety through interpersonal relationships. You just "know" the right thing to say or do in many situations. You know how to make others feel comfortable, and you can choose your words wisely to achieve your own purpose.

With practice you can pinpoint the source of feelings coming at you more precisely, thereby using your ability to formulate conscious plans of action. You can also develop your imagination into a storytelling ability, using the stories to illustrate your feelings or to influence the decisions of others. Or the story-telling can become a significant element in your career. People love good stories and respond to them with action appropriate to their content. You learn to capitalize on this human quality.

The Midheaven in Libra

Beneath the subconscious desire to engage actively in whatever attracts your attention, you find the desire to devote yourself to someone or something outside yourself. You may experience an initiation with a teacher to whom you devote yourself with single-minded faith and courage. You will benefit from practicing meditation, as you must clear your conscious mind in order to reach the profound state of consciousness where pure devotion arises. In the process of identifying a purer form of devotion you may appear fanatical in your actions or statements. You work with the forces of nature, striving not to control them but to flow with them naturally. The most positive attitude you can cultivate is one of harmlessness—you seek to do no harm and to think no evil.

Your understanding of the nature of duality in the world can be used to move past mere devotion to teacher. You will seek an attitude that engenders the fusion of body and soul, with its illumination of the ideals of unity in your spiritual life. You learn the meaning and value of self-sacrifice, not because they are goals in themselves, but because they will lead you to an understanding of higher spiritual service on the group level.

To understand your own core beliefs is to live in harmony with your spiritual being. These beliefs emerge from the deepest part of your being. When studied, they provide the information for a lifetime of self-exploration.

The Midheaven in Scorpio

Beneath the subconscious desire to establish comfort and stability in your life, you find the capacity to see the dimensions of spiritual life. You experienced limitations to your comfort in childhood, and you learned how family members expressed their desires, and in addition, how they sought to fulfill those desires. You were also able to observe how the selfish desires of one person caused pain and unhappiness for someone else. In this way you began to understand the duality of existence more objectively.

Out of this greater objectivity you learned the value of engaging your mind in thoughtful examination of situations, instead of leaping in with your naked desires. You have a profound capacity for sublimating your desires to a greater good, whether it be personal, social, or spiritual. When you seek to satisfy your physical, sexual desire alone, you feel disappointed in the result. When you instead seek a spiritual union with your partner, you discover an ecstatic state in which your souls merge, resolving and transcending the apparent duality of the physical plane.

The Midheaven in Sagittarius

Beneath the subconscious desire to be the arbitrator of conflicts in your life, you find the capacity to achieve resolution, both within yourself and among others, through more conciliatory means. You examine situations from an early age with an eye to how they are resolved, who is a skilled mediator, and how they find the middle ground and convince others to be flexible. You may study history and politics, or you may focus on sociology or psychology, depending on the direction of your interests.

Your understanding that all difficulties are largely a result of misunderstanding or lack of information can grow into an ability to serve others through diplomacy and tact on one hand, and through detailed examination of the factors involved in a problem. You have the makings of a researcher into profound subjects, as you believe in examining the source of a situation, and not merely the apparent symptoms.

The Midheaven in Capricorn

Beneath the subconscious desire to be comfortable with your present belief system, you find the desire to create conditions that provide for the transformation from a being driven by instinct to a person governed by intellect. The Moon combines its energy with other planets to bring this change about, so the Moon's aspects will have an important impact on how this change is wrought. In childhood you may simply absorb and accept the beliefs—and thereby act on the instincts—of your family. As you complete your childhood and begin adult developmental processes, you will find that not every basic belief of your family suits your individual needs. You then apply your mind to discovering what will work better for you.

You have a fluid mind and are able to retain what you have been taught while at the same time motivating yourself through new experiences. Because you are listening for the nuances of your soul, you find the proper direction for your own activities, and you do this without needing to break the mold provided by your family and social position. When the intellect has been fully engaged, you will move into the rich experience of intuition, and you will be able to foresee the results of your decisions and plan even more responsibly.

The Midheaven in Aquarius

Beneath the subconscious desire to "rule the roost" in your home, you find a melding of love and wisdom that serves as a beacon for all your activities. All the factual information that you gather from family members, through the educational system or personal study, and from interactions with spiritual teachers filters into your memory and combines with those beliefs and memories carried forward from previous lifetimes. Through experience with others, you develop the wisdom to make creative, beneficial decisions.

In addition to concrete information, you also store intuitive input concerning emotions. If your childhood was difficult, you may have problems engaging in loving relationships. You will benefit from an examination of beliefs that are inconsistent with your desire to have meaningful relationships with romantic or other partners.

The most creative attitude you can develop relates to the merging of heart and mind—seeing your world from both intellectual and intuitive perspectives and honoring both in all your dealings with others.

The Midheaven in Pisces

Beneath the subconscious desire to understand the minute details of physical existence, you find the capacity to experience the germination of your spiritual life. As a child you observed the way your parents and other people involved themselves with the details of their daily existence, and you learned how to manage your own activities with attention to specifics.

While you were learning the practical skills you needed for daily activities, a spiritual awareness was also growing deep within you. You have rejected the strict bonds of servitude on the material plane, yet you have cultivated the joyful possibility of spiritual service, even if you are only vaguely aware of this fact. You are learning that you can engage on the personal, thoughtful level in activities that help you and others, or you can expand your understanding to include a broader spiritual venue in which you transcend your ordinary mental boundary.

Midheaven Aspects

Connections between the Midheaven and the planets reflect your potential for self-awareness. The energy of the planet reveals a second component of consciousness that can challenge or enhance the natural tendency indicated by the sign the Midheaven occupies. Thus the aspects are tools unique to your personal chart, and therefore represent the skills you have as an individual to pursue higher spiritual aims and values.

Tools for Your Spiritual Quest

You are consciously aware of your own ambition. You know how to use what is close at hand to adapt to your environment. You are also aware, or can gain awareness, that your ambition is appropriate only when it supports the needs of the people around you. Harming others to achieve your needs will not further your spiritual development. Quite the opposite is true, in fact. It is part of your spiritual role to correct injustice where you find it.

You can become a master builder on the physical plane, creating something of lasting value. You do this by accessing the values you hold deep within yourself. The significance of emotions lies within you. Your inner voice can reveal each step on your path, not to master your emotions, but to become aware of their power. Mastery of emotion has the ring of eliminating them, or chaining them so they cannot interfere with your conscious efforts. Awareness of them, on the other hand, will allow you to use their power to help others. At that point you are no longer under the control of unconscious energy.

CHAPTER 11

MARS
Your Spiritual Persona

Mars indicates an area of life that is vitally important to your spiritual growth. Whatever path you choose, this factor will come up again and again, modifying your direction or suggesting a specific focus for your studies. This source of energy and spiritual guidance is a deeply personal and private part of your life. Others will see how it affects you, but they are unlikely to understand the depth of its significance. You yourself may not understand the power of this influence on your life, yet you experience its influence strongly when Mars is aspected by direction or transit.

Mars in the Elements

Mars is naturally associated with Aries, a fire sign. Traditionally Mars was also associated with Scorpio, a water sign. Thus the expression of Mars shares the nature of these two elements to some extent. In Buddhist psychology the relationship between water and fire is called *Padma*, and it involves the capacity for discriminating awareness. Mars governs the five senses—touch, taste, sight, hearing, and smell. The position of Mars directly reflects your capacity to relate to the world through your senses.

Mars also reflects your capacity to purify your system. On the physical level you have a fever when you are fighting off an infection. On the emotional level you feel like you have a fever when you are in the throes of sexual passion. Sometimes your work drives you to a feverish pitch. In the spiritual level you have an area of your life where you feel the fever as well. You devote yourself to moving forward and upward in your spiritual quest where Mars is found by element, sign, and house.

Mars in Fire

You naturally consider the future while taking action in the present. You relate to the physical world via intuition, and you do the same in spiritual considerations. When you encounter a dilemma or paradox in your life, you tend to project the problem into the future to hypothesize how it will be resolved, and then you take action in the present to move toward that outcome. Your actions, while focused on the future, are always a reflection of a purification process that is usually associated with water.

Mars in Earth

You are generally practical in your activities. If something has no hope of reaping actual, measurable results, then you just won't do it. This practical streak carries over into the spiritual realm as a desire to develop a regular practice that deepens your sense of devotion to a teacher or to a body of understanding about your true purpose. On the material level your actions are designed to help you acquire whatever you need, but also to acquire those material things that enhance your feeling of comfort and richness. On the spiritual level your devotional practice—prayer, meditation, good works—also focuses on a goal. Many teachers suggest that meditation has no goal, but in our culture you are almost certainly seeking something from whatever you do, including the spiritual direction you take.

Mars in Air

You are able to take an idea and wind it into an imaginative yet logical picture, filled with colorful images and connections. Your spiritual discipline is likely to reflect this strong use of intellect. You find causes to which you devote time and energy, and you are best placed in jobs or activities that draw on your mental capacity. Today's focus on the Internet and telecommunications suits your energy very well, as you are able to picture systems and to devise strategies for the future.

Mars in Water

You are like a steam engine in many ways. Once you get rolling, it is nearly impossible to slow you down. You are able and willing to push into territory that other people shrink from, and you come out of difficult situations more or less in one piece, with your enthusiasm intact. You exemplify the connection between the past and the future in your devotion to whatever task you set for yourself. You are not satisfied until this connection has been made and you understand it. Spiritually you have to understand your karma from the past in order to guide your present decisions. Thus you may press deeper into your personal and family history, and even into past lives.

Mars in the Signs

In addition to the house and element placement of Mars, the sign placement is significant to developing your spiritual persona. The sign colors the message you receive concerning the direction your spiritual path will take. For example, suppose you have Mars in Cancer in the Eighth House. Your nurturing, family-oriented persona (Mars in Cancer) is directly affected by a desire to help others improve their self-esteem and transform their lives (Eighth House). You may nurture by preparing healthy, enticing meals for your family and acquaintances. People may turn to you in times of crisis because they find you sympathetic, but more because they find you are able to help them.

I have listed three personality traits associated with each sign. If you consider each trait listed for the sign Mars occupies in your chart and consciously evoke it in your daily activities, you will find that the path becomes more fulfilling, more insightful, and easier. You will find that by actively devoting energy to the development of one trait, you spontaneously develop several traits associated with other signs.

Mars in Aries
Spontaneity, enthusiasm, courage

Mars in Taurus
Persistence, generosity, patience

Mars in Gemini
Tolerance, resourcefulness, mediation

Mars in Cancer
Veneration, inspiration, appreciation

Mars in Leo
Fairness, sacrifice, humility

Mars in Virgo
Discrimination, moral strength, unselfishness

Mars in Libra
Cooperation, honesty, impartiality

Mars in Scorpio
Regeneration and transformation, determination, healing

Mars in Sagittarius
Reverence for all life, open-minded attitude, cheerfulness

Mars in Capricorn
Concentrative power, self-control, faith

Mars in Aquarius
Group values, new ideas, memory

Mars in Pisces
Empathy, receptivity, adaptability

Mars in the Houses

Mars in the First House

Ideally you want to use your energy to move yourself along the spiritual path. Your own evolution is plenty for you to manage, so to some extent you may disregard the needs of others in your haste to progress. At some point you begin to shift your personal desires toward more spiritual aspirations. When this happens you find that movement is faster, detours are fewer, and you generally feel that your spiritual life is more closely aligned with your physical activities.

Mars in the Second House

The focus of your spiritual persona is on issues of giving and receiving. You work hard to learn how to accept gifts from others, and you work even harder to learn how to give the most appropriate gifts to others. The spiritual work here is extremely powerful. You learn that you are giving of the Universe and of yourself, freely and joyously. There is a strong moral sense to your life. You practice your principles each day.

Mars in the Third House

The focus of your spiritual persona is on issues of mind. Your educational zeal provides you with the staying power to delve deeply into subjects that interest you. You may become a writer or teacher because you feel strongly about your interests and want to communicate them effectively. You also are careful in the use of words, as you understand how deeply they affect others. If you can harness your own emotions, you can become an effective negotiator or mediator.

Mars in the Fourth House

The focus of your spiritual persona is on issues of family tradition. You may spend a lot of time sorting out the family beliefs that ring true for you from those that do not. You tend to develop a home environment that is conducive to your spiritual path. Your energy can become scattered when you don't have a safe harbor in which to develop your spiritual focus.

People show you the significance of your values on an energetic level. This could include angry disagreements, body language, or fluctuations on the subtler level of the aura. Their heat can act as a metaphorical barometer of your own intensity.

Mars in the Fifth House

The focus of your spiritual persona is on issues of creativity. Creativity has three parts: creation, recreation, and procreation. Your spiritual path is uniquely tied to these three expressions of your being. Therefore it is important for you to at least consider all three. You may not choose to have children of your own, but you are drawn to activities with young people. You probably will find that all your activities have a creative angle.

Mars in the Sixth House

The focus of your spiritual persona is on issues in the work environment. Wherever you find yourself, you seek the opportunity to provide spiritual sustenance for others, and to work out your own spiritual issues. You take a holistic view to your spirituality. No part of your life is separate from it (this is true for everyone). For you, however, the focus is on making your whole life into a consistent spiritual package. You then seek to help others achieve the same consistency.

Mars in the Seventh House

The focus of your spiritual persona is on issues of partnership. From childhood you have placed high value on close relationships. You demand a lot from an intimate partner, and you throw your energy into returning the favor. The partner is a mirror for your spiritual values, your feelings, and your expression. Your devotion to one special partner provides a path to service. Any contact with the general public is seen as a spiritual opportunity.

Mars in the Eighth House

The focus of your spiritual persona is on issues of death and transformation. You seek experiences that help you understand your own life and death cycle, with a desire to help others understand their own. A second issue that affects your path is your own sexuality. Physical desires can be very strong, and you need to develop judgment in this area of your life. Long-term relationships transmute physical sexual drives into spiritually ecstatic experiences that lift you to peak moments of understanding.

Mars in the Ninth House

The focus of your spiritual persona is on issues of education. You may seek to travel and experience the world, or you may pursue other educational objectives. You may eventually become a spiritual teacher. A second very powerful spiritual theme is your devotional path, which may include a formal religion, a return to far older traditions, or an eclectic gathering of spiritual experiences that contribute to your expanding consciousness.

Events that point to your transcendent values tend to have a combative component. There is energy to spare and you travel the world to find ways to use it. Desire is what drives you in your search for your unique set of values. You know you are unique, and you want to express that individuality on the spiritual level. The inner struggle is for self-mastery. You seek, beyond all else, to harness your energy for effective action. As you progress through life you find that less constructive traits, such as defiance, combative behavior, and egotism are transmuted into more refined expression of your devotion to your spiritual path, generosity toward others, and determination to make a positive impact in this lifetime.

Mars in the Tenth House

The focus of your spiritual persona is on issues of right livelihood. You will not be satisfied with any career that leads you away from the spiritual path. At the same time you devote your energy and time to becoming successful in your career. In the long run you seek to convert pride in your accomplishments into the achievement of spiritual goals for their own sake. You can become an exemplar of all that is best in your chosen career field.

Mars in the Eleventh House

The focus of your spiritual persona is on issues concerning the group process. You understand the ritual content of human interactions, and you can facilitate meetings by injecting the missing ritual pieces into any situation. You train your enthusiasm to always include tactfulness and kindness. You focus on the power of hope within yourself, and you can engender this emotion in others.

Mars in the Twelfth House

The focus of your spiritual persona is on issues hidden deep in the Collective Unconscious. You experience the upwelling of images that have affected people throughout history, and you seek to fit them into your spiritual perspective. Deeply introspective, you are able to listen to your inner voice and follow its urging. To the extent that you cultivate self-examination, you come to see the world as a container for your life, and not as an enemy to be fought against.

Summary

The combination of Mars and its house and sign placement form a picture of your application of personal energy where the spiritual path is concerned, and may be used as a benchmark to work with your own chart or the charts of clients. Remember, the indications are appropriate to a lifetime of spiritual development, and some facets may not be evident until later in life. They can be viewed as goals to strive for throughout your life.

Case Study: Muhammad Ali

Normally when someone proclaims that he is the greatest, we take that as a sign of his arrogance. We like to think that spiritual development brings with it a sense of humility. We do not find such a quality in Muhammad Ali without looking deeply into his life, and even then we may not be convinced.

Associating Ali with the energy of Mars is easy. He demonstrated that he was indeed the greatest fighter in many ways. How many of us remember spending money for a pay-per-view fight, inviting all our friends over for a party, and then seeing only a few minutes of action before Ali knocked out his opponent? How many of us can do *anything* as fast as he could throw punches? In a fight in London he was timed at seventeen punches in two seconds! He exemplifies the nature of Mars aggression on the physical plane.

Ali has Mars in Taurus. It is elevated—it is the planet closest to the Midheaven. Ali's chart is filled with very close aspects, and Mars is included among them. The square to his Twelfth-House Pluto has an orb of less than two degrees, and is the closest of the traditional aspects involving Mars. This indicates the intensity of Ali's power and his ability to apply that energy in the ring. The power comes from the Twelfth House—Ali gathers his power from a private place within himself.

This inner source of power is the first clue concerning his spiritual nature. He cultivates the inner voice and listens to it. His first regular fight was in 1954, when he was twelve years old. By solar arc Mars formed a trine to the North Node in the Second House of self-esteem, indicating that he was able to bolster his self-image from the opening moments of his amateur career. Solar arc Venus formed a sextile to the birth Mars, indicating an opportunity for him to show what he was capable of.

The solar arc aspect of Venus to Mars reflected the closest Mars aspect in the birth chart—the Venus quintile. Ali's talent lies in using his energy to promote his career (Venus rules Taurus, the sign on the Midheaven). Never a street fighter, Ali knew from a very early age that he wanted to concentrate his efforts in the single direction of professional boxing.

In the aspects section of this book, you will find the following description of Venus quintile Mars:

> Love is your best creative medium. This means that romantic partnerships, sexual fulfillment, and spiritual communion all can be used to develop creatively.

While Ali was very vocal about his prowess as a fighter, he was less vocal about his spiritual path. He was connected with the Nation of Islam, in a very private way, before his fight against Sonny Liston on February 25, 1964. Less than a month after that fight Cassius Clay announced to the world that he was now Muhammad Ali, a member of the Nation of Islam. When he faced Liston again about a year later, he achieved a knockout in the first round. Many people believed that Liston took a fall, but examination of the fight tapes shows that Ali may have landed a damaging punch that set up the knockout a few seconds later.

We all face tests along the spiritual path, and Ali faced one of his when he was drafted. The U.S. Army wanted to use him as a poster boy, keeping him out of combat, but Ali refused to be used by the establishment. How many of us would choose a jail sentence because of our spiritual beliefs? After the jail term Ali was able to come back to the fight game, but he had lost some of his incredible speed. He had a number of knockouts and wins after his comeback, including defeats of George Foreman in Zaire and Joe Frazier in Manila.

Whether you are in the camp of people who declare Ali to be the greatest athlete of the twentieth century or not, you can see that he had tremendous determination that carried him from age twelve through a twenty-eight-year boxing career. He was "in your face" to the news media and in the ring. In his private life he pursued his spiritual beliefs with comparable intensity.

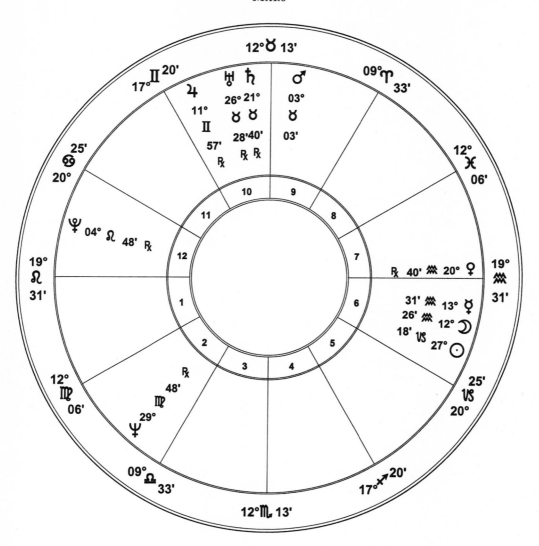

MUHAMMAD ALI
January 17, 1942 / Louisville, KY / 6:35:00 P.M. CST
85W46'00"   38N15'00"

Case Study: Saint Augustine

Saint Augustine has Mars in Leo. Born in 354 C.E., he was an early Christian convert who made this religion his life. He thought deeply about his own life and about his future life after death, and he applied his moral and ethical values in his work. But it was the Holy Spirit that seemed to light him on fire, and it was this spirit that guided the rest of his life. His mother was a Christian, but he was not baptized until the year 386, when he converted from the heretical beliefs of Manichaeism.

Augustine wanted to pursue philosophy. When he read books on Neoplatonism, he found a philosophy that meshed with his Christian beliefs. He then determined to pursue "truth," which he associated with Christianity. His blending of the philosophical side of his religion with the popular beliefs of his congregation resulted in the framework of theology that survives in both the Roman Catholic and Protestant branches.

Unfortunately, it is in his writings that Pope Gregory found the justification for the Inquisition, and it is Augustine's views that were used to justify the attitudes of the Christian Right in the late twentieth century. Principally, the view Augustine put forward is that it may be necessary to deprive people of their rights at first. The logic is that people can be forced to "attend the feast" so that they can understand its value. Later they can be free to make their own decisions.

Augustine himself was a judge, and the record of his court indicates that while he may have preached a hard line, he actually took a more merciful stance with his own rulings. This is consistent with Mars in a fire sign, as Augustine had one eye on the person before him and the other eye on the future. He used his intuition to guide his decisions, while using scrupulous logic in his writing.

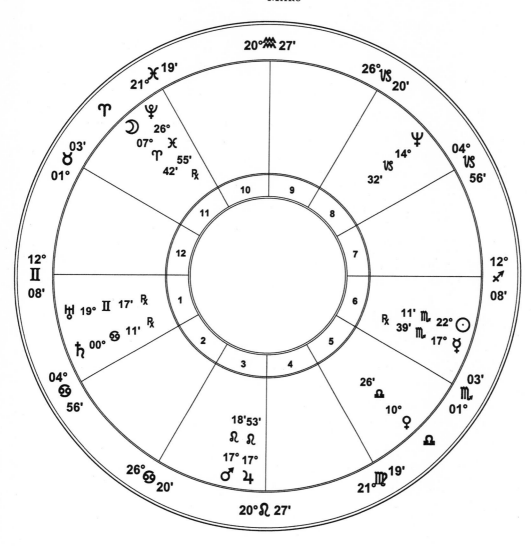

SAINT AUGUSTINE
November 13, 354 / Souk Ahras, Algeria / 6:00:00 P.M. LMT
8E00'00"   36N23'00"

CHAPTER 12

THE ASCENDANT
Expressing Spirit in the World

The Ascendant provides a personal anchor for understanding spiritual potential and process in the birth chart. From a transpersonal perspective—a viewpoint from outside the individual personality—we are reflections of the Sun, but we gravitate toward the Ascendant in terms of how we express ourselves in the world. This is because the rising sign represents choice—we can choose what we want to show to the world. Ultimately, however, we all come back to the Sun sign on the spiritual level. We are born with the purpose to express the Sun sign's spiritual values to the best of our ability, and we will come back to those values in the end.

Each person learns about the Sun sign's higher spiritual values and cultivates those values through developing the positive traits of the Ascendant. Each sign as it rises brings to light different personality traits, a different physical appearance, and a different sense of spiritual direction. The rising sign offers a container for our experimentation with constructive, creative personal choices about how to act in the world. Later we can take this practice back to the Sun sign and master its lessons.

The following section describes each sign as it rises. Remember that the Midheaven and Ascendant depend on an accurate birth time. If you don't know your exact birth time, this material may help you focus on a desirable set of traits to develop—you can develop a spiritual persona for yourself even if you don't know your time of birth. You may gravitate to one sign or another, thus indicating your approximate birth time.

The Ascendant in the Signs

The Ascendant in Aries, Ruled by Mars

Aries is the first sign of the zodiac. It expresses the will to power, but its primary expression is the unfoldment of potential—the power to manifest in the physical world. You are expressing the power to create on the material plane, but you are also capable of expression on the intuitive level. You understand the capacity of intuition to illuminate your life and the lives of others.

During your life you will find yourself going through cycles of intuitive insight and more practical application. All intuition without practical effort carries little impact, so you have to learn a compassionate style for delivering your psychic messages. With Mars as its ruler, Aries is not known for its compassion, so you have an interesting task. Qualities that you can easily demonstrate are your endless enthusiasm for life, your quick wit, and your spontaneous responses. Practice being enthusiastic about other people's paths—inject humor into difficult situations to ease their paths. And don't withhold your true response to their sadness and pain. If you are impatient, be impatient to see them reach the next level of creativity. If you are foolish, be foolish with your willingness to help. If you are jealous, show it as protectiveness of their tender hearts.

As you practice the strengths of your rising sign, you will find that what began as a lively, expressive personality is developing into your soul expression. For Aries the shift is from "I am" toward "I aspire to become." You aspire to become the container for intuitive truths that you can act on for yourself, and also share with others. You know, deep within yourself, that intellect functions best when it is paired with intuition. As you open yourself to the world of intuition, your sensitivity deepens. You become an active participant in the creative process as you reorient yourself toward your inner voice.

As you activate the purifying process of fire in your life, you may find that your physical health is affected. Wholeness and wellness are significant factors in your spiritual quest. The head, and especially the eyes, become the focus of your intuition and expression. When spiritual energy first arises, you may experience headaches and your eyes may tire easily. You may benefit from meditative practice in which you visualize energy moving up your spine and out the top of your head. See it flow around you like a fountain, to be pulled up your spine again. In this meditation you use the energy within you to move through any pain in your eyes or head, and you also can use it to connect with the immediate environment.

The Ascendant in Taurus, Ruled by Venus

From the spiritual perspective you are expressing the power of desire on all levels of your being. On the subjective level you are able to communicate the intensity of your passion, whether it be in terms of your career, your relationships, or any project you undertake. You believe there is no point in doing something unless you do it well, and you strive for perfection in every area of your life. At the same time, you are constantly aware of your comfort zone, and may shy away from activities that present difficult challenges.

Throughout your life you will develop a personal style for expressing your desires, perhaps learning to moderate them, or perhaps learning more and more skillful means of satisfying them while also presenting a socially graceful face to the world. At the same time your spiritual yearnings lead you to the best expression of your being on this higher level. Finally, you learn to direct your will so that all efforts satisfy both your material desires and your spiritual aspirations. You may find from time to time that you are faced with this question: Are my actions being driven by material desires, or am I following my spiritual aspirations? The answer helps refine your awareness of your deepest motivations.

Proper care of the physical body is important for your spiritual expression. As you emphasize the wholeness and wellness of the physical body, you metaphorically focus on the wholeness and wellness of your spiritual being.

The neck and throat become a powerful physical focus for your expression. Because proper speech is so important to you, the organs of speech and the thyroid gland are your most valuable physical attributes. Voice training or other attention to the throat and throat chakra may be important to your development of clear communication. But first you need to listen, to others and to your inner voice.

You have the capacity to understand the duality of the material world and to penetrate the paradoxes that arise in your life. You can learn to see the ebb and flow of energies in your inner experience and in the outer world, and you understand that the attraction and repulsion of these energies leads to eventual synthesis. You perceive that sexual desire is one expression of duality on the physical level. The power of this duality provides the impulse to transcend mere physical desire and to discover the mystical union of forces. As you gain in experience, your sexual expression may deepen into the ritual of Tantra. Then you will feel the blossoming of spiritual awareness on a higher vibratory level.

Perhaps the greatest challenge you face is the transmutation of knowledge into wisdom. You have to develop spiritual awareness in order to go beyond stubborn attachment to personal desires. Your temper will give way to spiritually directed effort. Blind pursuit of self-interest will give way to a spiritual focus. Self-pity will give way to a concern for all humanity.

The Ascendant in Gemini, Ruled by Mercury

Gemini is able to express dual natures on the ordinary plane and in your spiritual life. There is a magnetic quality to your personality that attracts others to you, but that may cause periods of indecision. For example, you may determine that you want to adapt your spiritual path to suit your personal needs and desires, but are unsure of which path to pursue. It may be essential for you to study two or more practices in order to fine-tune them to your personal vibration. Often the best path is one that integrates several methods. However, before you begin the tuning process, learn the basics of each individual discipline first. In this way you will see the similarities and differences clearly.

Mind training is helpful for the Gemini Ascendant. Mind training includes exercises in cognitive thinking—training the mind to engage before emotion carries you away. It allows you to mediate between your inner life and the outer environment. As you experience the boundary, you begin to refine your beliefs about the nature of any separation you perceive. You also learn to relate between your lower self (personality) and your higher self (soul), so that you more readily express the soul's nature to the world.

The finest skills of the mediator lie in the capacity to bring opposing factions together. Your life is spent developing a keen sense of duality—you sharpen your perceptions through such distinctions. Then you are able to flow into the perception of Unity, and you become a messenger for the truth. Because there can be only one Truth in the world, you serve to show opponents in an argument just how their separate "truths" are part of one larger whole.

The Ascendant in Cancer, Ruled by the Moon

Cancer is the first of the water signs. On the material level it reflects the group energy of humanity, so you are able to both feel the energies of other people and experience the flow of energy within yourself. It is this capacity to feel that gives rise to the nurturing side of this sign. The sign Cancer reminds us of water flowing downhill. It is the relentless quality of the flow that you resonate with. Even when you feel stuck in situations, you can identify the "flow" that continues among the individuals involved and around the objects in your environment.

Much of your feeling experience occurs on the soul level. If you see auras, you may see all the way to the soul level of the person. This can be both informative and frightening, as you may not wish to relate that closely with everyone. If you don't actually see auras, you certainly feel the energy of other people and need to have inner clarity so that you can interpret those signals correctly. Therefore it is important for you to have a spiritual practice that is designed to cultivate clarity of mind.

Movement is a key principle in your life. How you begin the digestive process, for example, determines what you are able to assimilate from your food. The movement of fluids through your body is a familiar and comfortable barometer of your moods. Good spiritual practice may focus on movement as well. Walking meditation may be helpful for you. If you feel stuck, strenuous exercise may help shake loose whatever is bothering you. Then you can return to a more meditative pace of movement. Follow movement with sitting for a few minutes to experience the inner calm that has been strengthened.

As you experience your spiritual being, you come to understand the two sides of the sign of Cancer. One side has to do with self-preservation and includes the nurturing you receive and the care you give to others. It includes the impulse to incarnate in the first place. The other side relates to immortality. Your creative energies are freed as you gain understanding of this aspect of life. By understanding the desire to incarnate, along with the truth of your immortal being, you perceive the flow of the evolutionary process across physical lifetimes. The mystery here is the link between the Mother of Form (the Moon) and the Father of the Waters (Neptune). On the physical plane, form is not necessarily rigid, and movement is not necessarily unrestricted. The two aspects are intertwined in all living things. On the spiritual plane, form may seem less significant or less solid, but the principle of form continues to be active until Unity is achieved.

The Ascendant in Leo, Ruled by the Sun

The first four signs incorporated the seed of intuition, the desire for expression, the capacity for thought, and the depth of feeling and potential for reproduction. Now, with the Leo Ascendant, you experience the capacity of will. For the plant kingdom, will expresses in the ripening of the fruit. Will, for us, is the drive to creativity in the material world, and aspiration on the spiritual plane.

You only need to observe the activities of children between the ages of ten and twelve or thirteen to understand the power of will. At their best they are fully engaged in life, seeking a wide range of experiences, and creatively interacting with their peers. They are testing their wills against those of parents, teachers, and acquaintances. They are learning how to manage the force of will that drives them. There is a blending or fusion of all life's experiences for this age group that reflects the energy of Leo on the Ascendant quite well. Leo will gather information on the intuitive plane, measure it against what is perceived through the physical senses, and then mobilize the spirit behind whatever action is taken. This process results in a degree of self-consciousness that was not there previously.

The focus of physical energy is on the heart and the spine. Clear intuition often comes through the heart center, and clear effort depends on mental and emotional structure like that of the spine. The two need to work together to accomplish anything on either the physical or spiritual level. Perhaps the most powerful piece of writing I have encountered that speaks to the fusion of intuition and will is the Heart Sutra. This Buddhist text is a short poetic expression of the true nature of things. The complete text is included in the appendix. Here I wish to include a couple of thoughts:

1. "Form is emptiness and the very emptiness is form." This basic statement incorporates the paradox of existence in its basic form. It is possible for the Leo Ascendant to grasp the nature of the paradox and make it the spiritual guide for the Will.

2. The mantra, or spell, included in the Heart Sutra is as follows:
   (Gate is pronounced gah'tay)

Gate	gate	paragate	parasamgate	bodhi svaha.
Gone	gone	gone beyond	gone altogether beyond,	O what an awakening, all-hail!

Because the mantra is from Sanskrit, reciting in the native language may have more power (this is probably true of all spells and mantras). However, the English translation retains both the rhythm and the "g" sounds that are integral elements of the mantra. Imagine a room full of monks repeating the mantra in their deep voices. The mantra is heard, but the vibration also affects the heart directly.

The Ascendant in Virgo, Ruled by Mercury

The most pervasive trait of the Virgo Ascendant is analysis. Because you have a choice in how to engage in Virgo expression, you tend to analyze everything you do with the intention of improving your own performance. You are able to research a subject intensely, studying the nuances of situations in order to find the most utilitarian methods for the task at hand. Once you have mastered a subject, you are well able to teach it to others in a logical, step-by-step way.

The developmental stage reflected in the Virgo Ascendant is the harvest. You rejoice in the moment when everything comes together in a fruitful expression of cooperation. You discriminate among factors presented to you and usually are able to find the proper line of approach to any problem. The less constructive side of the Virgo Ascendant can be seen in mental egotism. You sometimes feel you are superior to other team members, for example. You find fault with their work, perhaps in an attempt to show your superiority.

The path of Virgo is not easy. It embodies the human capacity to protect, to nurture, and to reveal higher spiritual truths. The developmental power of Virgo can be experienced on at least four levels:

1. First there is the mental capacity. You examine, experiment, and think about the results.

2. You use the same thought processes to examine emotional and astral realms, and understand the depth of personal involvement in this way.

3. You have the capacity for understanding the process of motherhood. You use all your practical skills to nurture your children, your crops, or your creative efforts through to maturity.

4. You metaphorically destroy or leave behind each task and its results.

The potential weakness of the Virgo Ascendant is spiritual materialism. You may be tempted to make your spiritual path into a measure of your value. Or you may measure your own spiritual value against that of another person. The aforementioned egotism and faultfinding may extend themselves into the spiritual world. This potential pitfall is part of the probationary quality of Virgo. In traditional astrology Virgo is the sign of service, and this is true on the spiritual plane as well.

The power of cycles underlies the spiritual path of the Virgo Ascendant. For example, the phases of the Moon hold tremendous power because through them Virgo can relate to the energy of the Earth itself. Sensitivity to the nuances of cycles can become a formidable force in your hands when you are open to their subtle movements. Contemplative practice helps you relax your mind so that natural cycles can be more easily perceived. You may have different practices for different cycles of the Moon.

The physical effect of your spiritual work can often be felt in the nervous system. When your path is clear you can expect to feel calm and collected. When the path is not clear, you may feel a range of responses from tightness in the abdomen, to general stress, to heightened anxiety.

The Ascendant in Libra, Ruled by Venus

In some ways your persona is the balance of an object at rest. Metaphysically you appreciate the space between activities, so your persona reflects that kind of calm. This contemplative expression indicates that you can achieve a balance between your physical life and your soul life. As you learn to work with duality in a conscious way, your persona becomes calmer and you are able to effect change in the world without stirring up the energy more than necessary.

The tendency to balance and calm is part of what makes you a welcome guest. You can be counted on to enrich conversation both by listening actively and participating with clear questions, ideas, and an occasional opinion. You cultivate harmony among the people around you, and thus make a strong team member who can be counted on to keep the goal in mind in the midst of discussion.

As your spiritual path unfolds, you find that your sexual and other material desires change. You are still a physical being with needs and desires, but your motivations take on the quality of spiritual aspiration. Instead of engaging in sex for the sake of sex, you seek partners who share a spiritual affinity that allows you both to experience ecstasy through your relationship. Sometimes this even means engaging in activities that transcend the physical realm without using physical contact as the avenue of approach.

Sometimes we see an older couple hanging out together. They don't seem to talk very much, but we can see that they are attuned to each other. They investigate whatever catches the eye, pointing out things to each other. They are calm, not rushing their activity but following its natural pace. The outer appearance reflects an inner spiritual attunement that is the hallmark of the Libra Ascendant.

Libra Ascendants are vulnerable to any excess that throws the physical body out of harmony. This can result in a variety of ailments involving the kidneys, the bladder, and the sexual organs. You can enjoy life best by exercising a degree of moderation. In this way you demonstrate respect for yourself and your partner on the physical and spiritual level.

The Ascendant in Scorpio, Ruled by Pluto

You have already taken a few steps on the spiritual path, and you have dedicated your life to your spiritual nature to some degree. The intense desire nature within you continues, however, to pull you toward physical expression. You constantly find yourself at a turning point between pursuing a material desire and following a more spiritual inclination.

You have the capacity for major changes in your life. Others may find your decisions remarkable, as you can take a 180-degree turn with relative ease. Each of these major shifts brings you closer to understanding the unfolding plan of your spiritual life. At this time you may appear to be motivated only by material desires, but each turning takes you further on the spiritual path. If you look back, you can see that your decisions have all blended into one direction. You see the logical unfolding of spirit woven into seemingly disjointed actions and decisions.

First you test your physical appetites with food, sexual desire, and physical comfort. These may become rather boring. Ambition and the desire for power increase the emotional thrill and the momentary payoff. At the third stage you tackle mental challenges of spiritual pride. If you can transcend all three levels, you then function from a more spiritual base. You cease to seek physical emotional and mental thrills for their own sake, and use your personal power to transform your own life and to help others.

You face a tall order if you are to make spiritual progress. You need to remember your own beginnings as you seek success in any of your endeavors, spiritual or otherwise.

The Ascendant in Sagittarius, Ruled by Jupiter

You are driven by basic human motivations even when you pursue your spiritual life. Your rising sign, Sagittarius, governs the hips and thighs. It is the arrangement of these parts of the body that allows humans to stand upright and walk. Translate this metaphorically to your spiritual life—upright thinking and attention to your spiritual path are a reflection of your capacity to maximize human potential on the physical, emotional, mental, and spiritual levels.

In addition to the above capabilities, you have the capacity to use intuition in your life. You can envision the future better than most people. When you match your intuitive sensibility to your spiritual aspiration, you find that your path becomes easy to identify and to follow. The more you use your intuition, the more useful it becomes. Your intuitive ability rests in your intellectual development, so it is important to educate yourself well. In your studies you are often able to leap to the answer. It is important for you to fill in the blanks, even if it means going back, so that you learn how to solve more and more difficult problems.

You experience your soul's calling early in life. Other people may put down your budding ideas, but you gather these thoughts to yourself and nurture them. You trust that these ideas have come to you for some reason. You are able to recall them in moments of crisis, and you find you can communicate profound sentiments with few words. You have material ambitions, yes, but you also have spiritual aspirations. You will find that right spiritual aspiration often brings suitable material satisfaction in its wake.

Because your rising sign is connected to the hips and thighs, you may find that walking meditation, Tai Chi, or other contemplative movement suits your spiritual development. Sitting may not help you focus, while walking meditation may allow your thoughts to settle and your intuition to arise.

The Ascendant in Capricorn, Ruled by Saturn

Your rising sign's symbol is the goat, an animal that seeks the highest places on a mountain. The symbol also incorporates the tail of a fish, suggesting that your roots are somehow in the water. The part of the body related to this sign is the knee. Two images come to mind: you engage in the ambitious climb through your profession, seeking greater height for its own sake, yet you are able to dive into the water and use your flexible knees to move you through the water. The contrast of material upward progress and downward movement into the emotional realm is striking. Yet both are related to the material condition of the living human being.

Your spiritual path lies in the blending of these forces, and the material plane provides the catalyst for your spiritual development. One-sided material ambition cannot elevate you to a higher spiritual plane any more than a one-sided emotional life can satisfy you completely. Together they form the foundation from which all future progress emerges. It is from this synthesis that you can move into the next cycle of your upward moving spiritual path.

The hallmark of this rising sign is intelligent activity. Thus it is important for you to pay attention to whatever subjects you study and to go beyond the facts to discern the theory that governs your interests. Finally you will be able to use your skills to identify multiple solutions to problems. Then you can exercise spiritual discernment to identify the solution that best suits the situation and the individuals involved. Finding a workable solution is coupled with the desire for a harmonious solution.

Going back to the knee, the capacity to kneel parallels your ability to climb and to swim. I recall stories of pilgrims who travel the last part of their journey to a shrine on their knees as a sign of humility before the greatness of the divine. You may want to learn humility before the greatness of your peers and learn to serve them willingly.

The Ascendant in Aquarius, Ruled by Uranus

You pursue your spiritual path along three distinct lines:

1. Self-serving personal aggrandizement that shifts into the service of humanity.

2. Selfish attention to material superficiality that transforms into spiritual activity to serve a divine purpose.

3. Self-conscious activity on the interpersonal level that changes to broader humanitarian awareness.

Each of these three tendencies is expressed in alternating activities, and it may be difficult to sort out what your lower and higher motivations are at any given time.

You have the capacity to think through situations. You can work with your physical desire motivations, your emotional attachments, and your mental processes to discern your typical behaviors and their motivations. As you do this, you encounter situations where your spiritual motivation is paired with a self-serving method. When this happens, you have the opportunity to change your tactics.

It is the movement that is important, not the precise content or direction. Your rising sign governs the circulation of blood through your body. Allow the metaphor of circulation to pervade your interactions with others and your communion with yourself. Permit the possibility in all your activities that your perceived goal is not the end of a process, but simply a milestone along the larger path.

The Ascendant in Pisces, Ruled by Neptune

The symbol for your rising sign is two fishes, bound together but moving in opposite directions. These fish represent your soul nature and your form nature. You have a form nature in order to experience the growth of your soul, yet the two can seem to struggle against each other. You find that pursuing your own personal material desires does not resolve this struggle, but only deepens it. You need to find a spiritual path that allows you both to satisfy your personal needs and desires, and to satisfy your spiritual yearning for significance.

How do you accomplish this balance? You can focus first on your instinctual nature. You find that you usually have a feeling about what to do in any situation, but you sometimes listen to other people instead of paying attention to your inner daimon. One way to allow this inner voice its say is to take time each day to isolate yourself and listen. Listening to the sound of water can focus your mind and let your inner voice be heard.

On the physical plane you are drawn to mediumship—your psychic senses perceive a lot that other people overlook. As you begin to listen more deeply, you find that your role is that of mediator between the seen and unseen worlds. You can sympathize with the difficulties of others, and you can synthesize the feelings and motivations that can help them. As you develop this skill, you will find that you are no longer operating from the instinctual level, but now use your intellect to discern on both planes and to synthesize the information you gather.

Probably your major problem is your psychic sensitivity. You need to work with this ability on the intellectual level so that you can use it effectively, instead of being its victim. Your sign is associated with the feet. Forward progress involves learning how to walk, both physically and psychically, through the obstacles before you.

CHAPTER 13

ASPECTS

How Spiritual Energies Interact in Your Chart

ach planet, sign, and aspect has its ordinary expression on the physical plane. Each also has an esoteric, spiritual expression that we learn as we proceed on the spiritual path. Through the alchemical process of refinement, we are able to draw out the spiritual qualities that we most need as individuals. The aspects in your chart indicate how your life is defined and how its refinement will occur. The aspects also indicate the lowest expression of energy. Thus we move from the unconscious, potentially destructive influence, through the conscious, intellectual, and emotional levels of mind to a higher, hopefully purer expression of spirit. Each of us has a unique personal experience of the planetary energies, and thus the aspects work a special magic for each of us.

Astrological aspects show energy patterns in astrological charts. Transiting and progressed aspects reflect moment-to-moment, highly individualized potentials for the expression of positive intention in our lives. By understanding the planetary energies, and the nature of their interactions, difficulties are avoided and progress on the spiritual path is enhanced.

Physical Cues for the Aspects

We get indications all the time about how we are doing physically, and our physical body also shows us how we are doing on the emotional, mental, and spiritual levels. The aspects in your chart suggest ways to use physical feedback as a metaphor for spiritual direction. By paying attention to the physical, you acknowledge that your inner voice can deliver its message in a variety of ways, and you communicate the fact that you are ready to listen to what it has to say.

Conjunction

The physical cue to developing your conscious access to intuition is bumping into things. You find that you get bruises from hitting the corners of furniture or stub your toe. Try looking upon the bruises as an indication that you should relax and meditate, even if it is only for a few moments.

Opposition

The physical cue to developing your conscious access to intuition is feeling out of sorts, as though you are not fully in your body. Try looking on the disorientation as an indication that you should relax and meditate, even if it is only for a few moments.

Trine

The physical cue to developing your conscious access to intuition is sluggishness. You may feel you simply cannot do another thing. Try looking upon the sluggish feeling as an indication that you should relax and meditate, even if it is only for a few moments.

Square

The physical cue to developing your conscious access to intuition is that you continually have to go around things to get to your destination. You find toys, clothes, or even furniture in your direct path. Try looking upon the obstacle as an indication that you should relax and meditate, even if it is only for a few moments.

Sextile

You have the capacity to see opportunities coming. What looks like a challenge or problem to friends and family may be just the ticket where you are concerned—the ticket to a new development in your life. When opportunities arise, the main difficulty lies in choosing those that you truly wish to pursue, and letting others go by. Meditation can help you relax your mind so that the inner voice comes through clearly. That voice can often tell you if the "fit" is right, which can help you avoid getting sidetracked.

Semisextile

The physical cue to developing your conscious access to intuition is an irritation, like an itch, that cannot be satisfied by the usual means. Try looking on the irritation as an indication that you should relax and meditate, even if it is only for a few moments.

Quincunx

The physical cue to developing your conscious access to intuition is when you begin to feel ill. A cold, stomach ache, or flu symptoms may be an indication that you need to adjust your schedule to allow for a few minutes, at least, of meditation.

Semisquare

The physical cue to developing your conscious access to intuition is tension. As long as you ignore the tension in your body or postpone doing something about it, you are denying a part of your mind. Try looking on the tension as an indication that you should relax and meditate, even if it is only for a few moments.

Sesquisquare

The physical cue to developing your conscious access to intuition is agitation. When you feel the butterflies in your stomach, when you feel the floor drop out from under your feet, you know that it is time to listen to the inner voice. Try looking upon the agitation as an indication that you should relax and meditate, even if it is only for a few moments.

Quintile

The physical cue that intuition is coming into play is that you get a flash of a concrete image. It could be an archetypal symbol, or it could be an image of the color of paint you want for your living room wall. It is a future picture of a change you want or need to make in your physical environment. When you get such a flash of insight, it may be helpful to take a few moments to write it down. Then you can go back to the idea later, refreshing your memory by reading the notes. This kind of insight may fade if you don't record it.

Biquintile

You see an image of yourself in your mind's eye. When this happens, you perceive that you are different in some way, and the difference is a desirable outcome. As the intuitive insight comes to you, you may feel a bit unsettled, the way you feel when wearing new clothes for the first time. The sensation of newness is your cue that change is possible. This kind of insight can lead to change only if you encourage the impulse to move forward. It may help formulate an affirmation of the desire.

Septile

Sometimes you simply know that an event will occur. The feeling is similar to the sensation when you "plan" to remove your dinner from the oven—you "know" that it will smell a certain way, that you will feel the heat of the container, and that the colors will have changed. There is no altering the outcome. And you know that you will receive a confirmation of your intuition. While you may wish to affect the outcome or warn the people involved, it is helpful not to push, as such an effort will make very little difference.

Biseptile

You feel a change coming the way you can sometimes feel a change in the weather in your bones. You sense that the change will have some effect on you, even though the actual event may involve other people. You brace yourself for impact, sometimes the way you would for a shot in the doctor's office, sometimes the way you would when your dog runs up to greet you. You know there will be an impact, good or bad, and you prepare yourself for it. Sometimes you are able to warn others, but often you are aware only of the feeling, and not the specific time, place, or person who will be involved.

Triseptile

You feel a change coming within yourself. You are aware, perhaps, that other people cannot see the change, and that they will be aware of it only after the fact. They may believe you have made a sudden decision without giving it much thought, but you have known about the changes and thought about them a great deal. You may find that life's path feels smoother if you give other people hints during the thinking stage. That way they are not caught off guard by your moves. Considering that these changes are going to happen—that they are fated—you can prepare yourself and the people around you to the extent that you feel them coming and talk about them.

The Conjunction Aspect

The conjunction aspect defines the beginning and ending point of a circle. It represents the prominence of a particular point, focusing energy in one sign. Two planetary energies are united, magnified, and emphasized, each by the other. Conjunctions indicate a transition from one style of expression to another. The transition may reflect the transition from one lifetime to the next, or it may indicate a shift of spiritual focus during this lifetime. Even though you may not experience both an ending and a new beginning, they are both reflected within this aspect.

Planets in conjunction remind us of Unity. As we grow in spiritual awareness, we come to see that what once seemed like absolute endings and beginnings are actually points along a continuum of time, milestones of spiritual progress in our lives. When two planets are together in your chart, they serve as a special kind of beacon, focusing your attention on one aspect of your life and indicating where your spirit is likely to shine for others to see. It may be somewhat difficult to identify the planetary expressions as separate energies. Because unity is the ultimate goal, you may not feel impelled to study them individually, but it is helpful to gain an understanding both of the planets themselves and the nature of their interaction, as indicated by the aspect they form.

Planets in a conjunction rotate around each other and illuminate each other. They each express on the ordinary, exoteric level and on the spiritual, or esoteric, level. Thus at some times one planet will dominate the other, and sometimes the ordinary or spiritual expression will dominate. The dance produced by this interplay is the focal point for decisions to change your spiritual direction in life by ending one mode of expression and beginning another. There is a synthesis of two planetary energies going on all the time with conjunctions in the natal chart, and a temporary synthesis when planets are conjunct by direction or transit. Birth chart conjunctions present the same interchange of energies again and again throughout your life, and help you learn specific lessons. Transiting conjunctions provide special moments for learning, and you can choose to carry the lessons forward consciously. A similar dance occurs with the other aspects, according to their energetic natures.

Sun conjunct Moon: Spirit and soul express together in your daily life. You tend to a single-minded spiritual purpose, and may not experience the full richness of life on the physical plane. It is important for you to achieve a balance of physical and spiritual demands. Deep relationship with a partner is a profound spiritual path for you.

Sun conjunct Mercury: Common sense guides your daily activities, and this is just as true of your spiritual path. You study and evaluate what you are taught, and you apply your spiritual values in your daily work and play activities, not separating one from the other.

Sun conjunct Venus: Feelings of love pervade your spiritual life. Strong relationships with your partner, friends, and family provide a spark of spiritual activity deep within you. This spark can be expressed artistically or through social interactions.

Sun conjunct Mars: You devote yourself to each of life's experiences. If you can't do something wholeheartedly, then you may decide not to do it at all. You make spiritual progress through your own efforts, and may reach extraordinary heights.

Sun conjunct Jupiter: All of your activities have the potential to bring joy into your life, and the ebb and flow is important for you to understand. Your heart can expand to contain many possibilities, and you can also learn to let go of one successful experience in order to embrace another.

Sun conjunct Saturn: The structure of your spiritual experience includes understanding the nature of karma. You know that events and relationships come and go, and that you must make the most of each encounter. Much of your spiritual work is done when you are alone.

Sun conjunct Uranus: Your revolutionary attitude causes you to leave one spiritual idea and move to the next. You will benefit by retaining the value from the past while moving toward the future. You have an unusual knack for joining apparently disparate ideas into a logical whole.

Sun conjunct Neptune: Your spiritual sensitivity can create problems, as you are open to both creative and destructive psychic influences. Being open is not the problem. What you must develop is discrimination between helpful and harmful energies.

Sun conjunct Pluto: Your powerful spiritual values can be the source of your best and worst behavior. Arrogance is the least attractive of your powerful qualities. You must first rule your own desires. Then you can move forward without creating dangerous conditions for yourself.

Sun conjunct Node: Close associations with men create the atmosphere for spiritual co-operation. You learn as much from the ending of these relationships as you learn while in them.

Sun conjunct Asc: You are generally self-confident and you find self-esteem within yourself, not from others. You are likely to gain recognition, and you desire it.

Sun conjunct MC: You are closely aligned with your own self-awareness. You may feel that your very being is tied up in the activities that shape your life and career. Whenever you begin a new venture, you can take time to ponder the thought that you are not the new venture, but only its guiding force.

Moon conjunct Mercury: You have an active mind, and you have skillful methods for testing your assumptions against the world around you. Your judgment is good, even when you are in the midst of change.

Moon conjunct Venus: Your emotional intensity can cause the ending of a relationship before you have learned all the lessons. When you are able to work through conflicts with others instead of avoiding the pain by walking away, you find profound spiritual support.

Moon conjunct Mars: You tend to get excited about a new idea, run with it for a while, and then leave it for another idea. This approach keeps you from making steady progress. Develop the will to complete a study before you move on to something new.

Moon conjunct Jupiter: You are happy to consider new ideas, and you are also happy to end situations that no longer work for you. You can become embroiled in spiritual or religious conflicts if you do not resolve them first within yourself.

Moon conjunct Saturn: Self-control marks your spiritual path, just as it marks your practical daily interactions. You desire to understand each step in your spiritual development, and you carefully consider what to accept and what to reject from each experience.

Moon conjunct Uranus: Strong emotional tension marks the beginnings and endings you face. Your spiritual adventures incorporate excitability and a tendency to rely on instinct. You are willing to make sacrifices in order to progress on the path.

Moon conjunct Neptune: You can feel change coming long before it arrives. Occasionally you misjudge the nature of that change, but as you develop your psychic senses, you become a better judge of events. You live on the edge and expose yourself to negative influences if you aren't careful to make objective evaluations of others.

Moon conjunct Pluto: Your intense emotions can forge powerful spiritual bonds with others, but they can also cause violent outbursts and result in the ending of valued relationships. You don't give the same attention to the needs of others that you give to your own one-sided views.

Moon conjunct Node: You forge strong spiritual links with other people throughout your life. You also experience breaks with these people, and may then feel terribly alone. Relationships with women are spiritually charged for you.

Moon conjunct Asc: You tend to associate closely with women and they can help you in spiritual matters. You are adaptable and seek harmonious relationships.

Moon conjunct MC: What you know about yourself is deeply rooted in your psyche. You can dip into this well of information from time to time to get help with any problem that arises in your life. Your soul life is a major consideration in everything you do. A strong partnership is helpful to your spiritual growth.

Mercury conjunct Venus: You are able to express spiritual values in relationships, and you are able to make graceful entrances and exits. Your lighthearted exterior belies a depth of sensitivity. You tend not to push forward along the spiritual path, but instead wander a bit.

Mercury conjunct Mars: You use your powerful mind to help you through difficult transitions in your life. Rash actions can cause arguments and breakups. You take to the path of devotion with determination.

Mercury conjunct Jupiter: You take a common sense approach to your spiritual life, considering many ideas along the way. Dishonesty is not an option. Your successes build on each other and spiritual optimism grows.

Mercury conjunct Saturn: You approach each transition in your life objectively and logically, thinking through the details until you are satisfied with the outcome you foresee. Because you go through many separations, you come to value relationships while you have them.

Mercury conjunct Uranus: Intuition speaks to you about the future, so you are generally not surprised when changes occur. You can be of tremendous help to others because you are usually prepared. Too many activities can dissipate your spiritual strength.

Mercury conjunct Neptune: Your imagination takes you into wondrous realms of the subconscious, and this can cause a lack of clarity at key transitional points in your life. You have sympathy for others, as you feel their distress directly.

Mercury conjunct Pluto: Your powers of suggestion allow you to take others along with you for whatever spiritual ride you are on. Yet your argumentative nature can spoil your studies, as you begin to argue before you have all the facts.

Mercury conjunct Node: On the one hand you have a smooth, sociable nature that gets you in, and on the other hand you have a tendency to gossip that can end valuable relationships. The desire for the exchange of ideas provides you with plenty of spiritual material with which to work. Mercury conjunct Asc: Your attitudes toward other people are a strong hindrance or aid to your spiritual growth. The exchange of ideas with others is key to your developmental process.

Mercury conjunct MC: You tend to see harmony as something that can be obtained only after conflict. Certainly conflict can be resolved harmoniously. You may also want to look within yourself for areas where there has been no conflict to resolve. Here you will find a useful spiritual tool. You may change careers in pursuit of spiritual growth.

Venus conjunct Mars: Tantra is one path you will certainly want to try, but you will get into it and out and back into it a few times before you master the energy flows. Be discriminating in your choice of tantric partners.

Venus conjunct Jupiter: The pursuit of wisdom parallels the pursuit of love in your life. Any conflict in love relationships causes you to consider your spiritual values all over again. You may like the stage of falling in love with a spiritual idea so much that you choose to do it many times before you establish a solid foundation.

Venus conjunct Saturn: You are reserved. You don't jump into a spiritual practice any more than you jump into a love relationship. You may do best with a spiritual teacher who is much older or younger than yourself. You accept endings as a necessary part of life.

Venus conjunct Uranus: Once you find the spiritual teaching that suits you, you are totally and forever hooked into it. Until that happens, you may try a variety of religious or spiritual practices. When you are on the right path, beginnings and endings around you become cyclical milestones in the development of your personal belief system.

Venus conjunct Neptune: You tend to fool yourself where change is concerned. You thus are able to drift into and out of spiritual grace without even knowing it. Don't mistake erotic dreams for the energy of tantra. Distinguish your personal desires from the teaching itself.

Venus conjunct Pluto: You are the stuff of saints and martyrs because you engage in your beliefs with a fanatical desire to conquer anyone in your path. A physical love relationship can make or break your spiritual connection, depending on your ability to nurture the depth of feeling.

Venus conjunct Node: Generally you are adaptable, and thus accept changes in your life. Spiritually you adapt a new idea to your core beliefs without having to make a wholesale change. The wrong spiritual path causes you to become inflexible and harsh.

Venus conjunct Asc: You always seek harmony and are a welcome social guest for this reason. Artistic efforts may be central to your spiritual process.

Venus conjunct MC: While it is good to think well of yourself, it is a mistake to become conceited about your accomplishments or looks. Recall the feeling of falling in love and apply it to all your activities, spiritual or otherwise. Love may hurt, but it also inspires your spiritual process.

Mars conjunct Jupiter: You find that most beginnings and endings in your life are fortunate, and you are able to extract the spiritual lessons successfully. Occasionally you rebel and run away from a lesson that could have been very informative.

Mars conjunct Saturn: Generally you feel that endings and beginnings are the pits. When you see the end coming, you resist, and when you feel some new idea about to take hold, you resist. Your life of resistance prevents you from the rate of progress you deserve, and you need to lighten up.

Mars conjunct Uranus: Like certain Christian saints, you tend to accidentally fall into the spiritual experiences you need. This could be through a physical accident, or it may be that your intuition and energy bring you to the proper crossroads again and again.

Mars conjunct Neptune: Weakness of physical or spiritual strength early in your life tends to push you toward the lessons you need to learn. Indeed, you get help at the right moments that carries you forward on the spiritual path. As you gain experience, you take on the planning of your path as a conscious effort.

Mars conjunct Pluto: At some point in your life you may feel that the gods or goddesses step in to impose changes on you. What you make of these moments determines your spiritual future. Generally, whatever effort you make will be well worth your time.

Mars conjunct Node: Cooperation becomes dispute and separation, and results in a new cooperative effort. This cycle will repeat itself until you focus on the desire to cooperate and develop a spiritual value system you can share with others without becoming dogmatic.

Mars conjunct Asc: You are a fighter, even in the area of spirituality. You are strongly attracted to success, and can become aggressive in your spiritual quest.

Mars conjunct MC: You apply your energy to understanding yourself as much as you apply it to career and other activities. Action and the desire for success are a big part of your life. Determination could be your middle name.

Jupiter conjunct Saturn: Patience is the key ingredient to management of change in your life. You have survived many previous changes, and your spiritual future will doubtless include some more. You make progress in seclusion.

Jupiter conjunct Uranus: You love your freedom, and will end relationships that threaten it. The right spiritual path for you allows you to approach the material world intuitively and wait for the right moment to make important decisions.

Jupiter conjunct Neptune: Your speculative mind takes you into and out of spiritual debates without too much friction. You tend to be rather idealistic about your spiritual choices, and can be disappointed in individuals who don't live up to your high standards. Ending such a relationship may be felt as a profound loss.

Jupiter conjunct Pluto: You desire to be the teacher, and you may chafe under the tutelage of a spiritual guru. Ego is the obstacle. Spiritual progress is generally not compatible with a desire to rule over others. Yet you have within you the makings of a great leader. Balance of desires is the key to success.

Jupiter conjunct Node: Your life is filled with meetings with people who can help you along your spiritual path. It will be your own lack of social skills that causes such relationships to end badly. Tact will serve you in the beginning and at the end.

Jupiter conjunct Asc: You have many successful associations that further your spiritual thinking. You are generous with your time and energy.

Jupiter conjunct MC: You tend to be optimistic and content. You attain success and spiritual growth through self-awareness. You seek to portray yourself as a kind, compassionate being.

Saturn conjunct Uranus: Life's cycles seem to be filled with difficulties. You may tend to rebel against your spiritual teachers. Use your will to get through the sudden turns of events, and develop the ability to roll with the waves of life's fortunes.

Saturn conjunct Neptune: Change causes you suffering that you must learn to accept if you are to make progress. You struggle between your human and spiritual natures, and slowly achieve success through the experience of suffering.

Saturn conjunct Pluto: You can be cruel, and thus you cause relationships to end far before their time. Balance your severe demeanor with silent activity in which you cultivate a spiritual attitude that allows compassion to show through.

Saturn conjunct Node: You tend to isolate yourself, especially when you are hurt. Working with an older person helps develop the capacity to cooperate, even in the midst of major change.

Saturn conjunct Asc: You prefer to associate with your elders, and you gain spiritual maturity early in life. You learn from experience—your own and that of others.

Saturn conjunct MC: Responsibilities weigh on you until you feel they are the only important thing in your life. Seek to establish the structure of your being so that responsibilities take their proper place among your many activities.

Uranus conjunct Neptune: Your psychic awareness places you at many crossroads, and you are well informed about which path to take. Still, change is not easy for you. You feel losses deeply. You may sometimes become confused about which path to take.

Uranus conjunct Pluto: Transformation suits you very well, and the changes that come your way are easily absorbed, as long as the other people involved are not emotionally upset. Plan your entrances and exits with other people in mind.

Uranus conjunct Node: You thrive on new situations and ideas. The desire for change may interfere with the complete assimilation of valuable spiritual lessons. You learn about change through your dreams.

Uranus conjunct Asc: Your intuitive sense of position sometimes places you in the center of the storm. Your spiritual development may be interrupted more than once.

Uranus conjunct MC: Change is the name of the game in every area of your life. You gradually learn to foresee change as you develop your intuitive capacity. Then life achieves greater equilibrium. Career movement can enhance your spiritual growth.

Neptune conjunct Pluto: Change provides treacherous ground for your spiritual development. You need to stick to the straight and narrow path of spiritual evolution, and avoid drugs, obsessions, and fraudulent activities.

Neptune conjunct Node: A certain rigidity in your personality can keep you from making smooth transitions. Your best spiritual exercise is conducted in private, where you need only rely on yourself.

Neptune conjunct Asc: Mystical values pervade your relationships. You are surrounded by glamour. Imagination fires your personality.

Neptune conjunct MC: You feel as though you don't have a clue about what is happening around you. This is not the case. You actually have many psychic clues. Work on sorting them out so that you can see the path before you.

Pluto conjunct Node: You share your destiny with other people, and this includes the major beginnings and endings of your life. Karmic associations govern your relationships to a large degree.

Pluto conjunct Asc: Powerful learning occurs each time you are faced with birth, death, or other changes in your life.

Pluto conjunct MC: The power to transform your life is evident in everything you do. This same power transforms what you know about yourself on a day-to-day basis. You can manage any career you undertake.

No conjunctions: The lack of conjunctions in your chart indicates that your spiritual interests are diverse. Treat each facet of your spiritual life with equal respect, and take your lessons where you find them.

The Hard Aspects
The Opposition, Square, Semisquare, and Sesquisquare

The aspects in this group are made up of 45-degree multiples, and are traditionally called "hard" aspects. They all involve situations in which action in the outer environment affects you as an individual, whereas the "soft" aspects indicate situations where conditions surrounding you can be acted on to your benefit.

The opposition aspect divides the circle into two equal parts. The polarity of the opposition focuses your spiritual life in a black-and-white sort of way. This can result in periodic dilemmas about how to proceed, or it can bring apparently disparate views into focus so that you can achieve a synthesis. The direct path between the planets is through the center, or through yourself. Learn to measure the polarities in your life internally, rather than depend on an objective view of them outside yourself. In this way you become more connected with the world around you, and you can more deeply understand the spiritual implications of divergent ideas. The symbol of the Tao reflects the fact that apparent opposites have the essence of the other within their own core. Because each planet is a different energy, not opposite to any other planet, it is the apparent polarity that provides the ground for spiritual lessons.

From the spiritual perspective, the lesson is discriminating awareness. The opposition presents the situation. You must become aware, and you must provide the discrimination. How do these two energies relate to your spiritual path, and how can you resolve the differences into a synthesis of thought and feeling? What is the value in the lesson? And how are your perceptions about the life of the spirit changed when you examine the dilemmas in your life?

The square aspect, 90 degrees, defines one quarter of the chart and connects signs of the same mode—cardinal, fixed, or mutable. The squares indicate challenges. They take you out of your inner spiritual world and thrust you into the world of people and events. And action. They can be seen and measured by others fairly readily.

The semisquare (45-degree) and sesquisquare (135-degree) aspects are part of the same harmonic as the opposition and square. They indicate your internal response to the outer pressures of life as indicated by the planets in the aspect. It is often difficult for other people to perceive the effect of a semisquare or sesquisquare. With these aspects your felt response is all they have to go on.

The Sun in hard aspect to the Moon: You are aware of the apparent differences between spirit and soul as they express in your daily life. You often struggle to decide what activities are the best for you personally, and you may even try to make this decision for other people from time to time. A companion on the spiritual path can be very helpful.

The Sun in hard aspect to Mercury: Common sense tells you that your material and spiritual lives are vastly different. Common sense can also be your guide to understanding them as part of one unified process. Use your daily work and play to integrate your transcendent values into every part of your life experience.

The Sun in hard aspect to Venus: Strong sexual urges may feel very separate from your spiritual leanings until you see sexual expression as part of your higher purpose. Indiscriminate sex will retard spiritual development, as it denies the higher value of this part of your human experience. Tantric practice can elevate sexual desire into spiritual ecstasy for you.

The Sun in hard aspect to Mars: You have tremendous physical energy that can be applied to the pursuit of spiritual goals. Put your best effort into each of your life activities, all the while keeping the spiritual component in mind. By engaging your heart completely in each act, you come to understand spiritual unity more fully.

The Sun in hard aspect to Jupiter: You find great joy in life and are also aware of the depths of sadness and other feelings. As you take the spiritual path, you begin to see these less as opposites and more as part of a continuum of feeling. When you can bring higher values to bear in both joy and sadness, you achieve a synthesis of possibilities.

The Sun in hard aspect to Saturn: You perceive the structure of your life as restrictive unless you can infuse spiritual values into all your activities. Early on you resent the authority of the church or teacher, but later you come to appreciate the ritual patterns of prayer, yogic practices, circle work, focused meditation—all life experience, in fact.

The Sun in hard aspect to Uranus: You are a rebel, and you see other people as the cause. In reality you are resisting your own inner voice, and may be projecting that onto others. If you can resist the urge to push people away, your intuition can begin to inform your approach to relationships. Then those hints about feelings become spiritual signposts on the path of awareness.

The Sun in hard aspect to Neptune: You are very sensitive to the feelings of others, and may confuse your experience with their feelings. You must discriminate between what you feel and how you judge the feeling in order to expand your psychic ability. Psychic awareness then becomes a gift in your interactions with others.

The Sun in hard aspect to Pluto: Your personal power can make you arrogant. If you believe you can use force to control others, then you turn away from higher spiritual values. Instead, develop awareness of power as a currency that flows between you and other people. Sharing it is essential in the pursuit of self-realization.

The Sun in hard aspect to the Node: Associations with males can provoke your awareness of spiritual development, or lack of it. But it is not your task to point out their shortcomings. Rather, you can encourage them on their path by encouraging yourself on yours.

The Sun in hard aspect to the Asc: Who you are and what other people see in you are very different. You undermine your self-confidence until you set your sights on spiritual values.

The Sun in hard aspect to the MC: Perhaps your biggest challenge in life is to act as though you are certain of your direction, while at each turning you are examining your own values and sense of self. Only after the fact can you be certain of your direction.

The Moon in hard aspect to Mercury: You are very aware of the flow of information. You understand how you take in new ideas, and also how you express them to others. As you assimilate new ideas on the spiritual path, examine how they mesh with your earlier life experience, and build on that foundation.

The Moon in hard aspect to Venus: Emotional and sexual intensity can separate you from spirit or bring you closer, depending on your awareness of the richness of the interactions you experience. The creative dynamics of two people merging is a profound source of spiritual awareness if you get past the physical tension and emotional conflict. This deepening of experience takes time.

The Moon in hard aspect to Mars: Emotional friction in your activities can make you feel separated from your inner being. Use your physical energy to push through emotional barriers by finding ways to work out feelings without hurting others. Stick with each feeling until you understand how it motivates you.

The Moon in hard aspect to Jupiter: You tend to place your faith in other people and this can make you gullible about their spirituality. Optimism is fine. Idealism is fine. Learn to discriminate based on both actions and words, and then look into your own heart to evaluate what you have seen. True spiritual values uplift everyone, not just a favored few.

The Moon in hard aspect to Saturn: You demand discipline from yourself, and you expect it in others. You may have had harsh teachers. Your spiritual path focuses on compassion for others, and you have to develop compassion for yourself as well. When others provoke fear in you, look also for the love they struggle to express.

The Moon in hard aspect to Uranus: Your strong intuition provides a rich source of information in your relationships with others. You may eventually be capable of seeing into the future quite clearly. Meetings with unconventional people can provide the spiritual contacts you need to make further progress. You can be a radical without being irresponsible.

The Moon in hard aspect to Neptune: You are deeply sensitive to the energies around you, and often know how others feel before they show any sign. Your spiritual gift is to be subtle in your interactions. Be compassionate but not gushy, and use your imagination to facilitate creative change in others, and within yourself.

The Moon in hard aspect to Pluto: Intense emotions are part of all your relationships. Your challenge is to become aware of which feelings are yours and which belong to others. Your spiritual life thrives in group activities if you learn to cooperate and not coerce change. Each interaction has the potential to transform your beliefs.

The Moon in hard aspect to the Node: Relationships with women are a huge factor in your spiritual life. You sense the deep well of values within each person you meet, and seek to understand it. Pay attention to how others express their values, and be selective about which ones you adopt as your own.

The Moon in hard aspect to the Asc: Women cause problems for you, but may also be the source of spiritual wisdom and inspiration.

The Moon in hard aspect to the MC: Women bring an emotional spotlight to your self-awareness. Among the tears and anger you find gems in the form of core beliefs that have been transformed to suit your present needs.

Mercury in hard aspect to Venus: Other people express their love in a multitude of ways, and you have the ability to compare their words to their deeds to determine how they really feel. You are hypersensitive to each word or nuance of action. A strong love union for you may begin in a lighthearted way, but takes effort to move to the next level.

Mercury in hard aspect to Mars: An argumentative style pervades your inner dialogue and may invade your interactions with others. Yet these people are able to help you develop your spiritual determination. Through them you will gain a broader range of judgment, making you a formidable voice for expressing spiritual values.

Mercury in hard aspect to Jupiter: You take an intellectual approach to relationships, and thus you learn spiritual values through listening and study. Develop your ability to speak clearly so that you can learn even more. Contemplative practice may help you focus your thoughts and become less absent-minded.

Mercury in hard aspect to Saturn: You seek people with whom you can engage in serious spiritual work. Your capacity to concentrate on ideas can develop into deep philosophical understanding. You may become a teacher for others, as you recognize the effort required and can inspire it in your students.

Mercury in hard aspect to Uranus: You have the capacity for telepathic communication. One way to work with it is to listen to messages, even if you can't associate them with anything practical in the beginning. By listening, and by sharing these experiences with others, you facilitate the flow of information to you from the larger universe.

Mercury in hard aspect to Neptune: You perceive the flow of feelings around you, and you are able to influence others when you focus your own feelings and send them out. Thus it is important to learn to manage and control your psychic intake and output. This ability may also serve you in your career, as you gain sudden insights in all areas of your life in much the same way.

Mercury in hard aspect to Pluto: Your restless mind is always turning up another piece of ground, searching for a revelation. You become irritable when others seem to withhold key information from you. Because you can easily influence others, it is important for you to decide which spiritual values you want to espouse.

Mercury in hard aspect to the Node: You find that your spiritual life moves forward in social and business settings. Thus, in your career it is imperative that you find work associates who share your values and who support your life path.

Mercury in hard aspect to the Asc: You tend to be critical of others. One of your hardest tests of compassion may be to lighten up. You can begin by softening your attitude toward yourself.

Mercury in hard aspect to the MC: When you experience inner tension, regard it as a sign that you can now receive or understand information about your core beliefs more directly. Tension, even agitation, can be a signal to stop for a moment to meditate. In this way you can open a channel to your inner voice.

Venus in hard aspect to Mars: Sexual passion can be refined into spiritual ecstasy, but only if you are willing to put in the time and effort to cultivate the deepest personal relationship with another person. You achieve spiritual growth in a relationship that has a sexual spark, but that also has the promise of a long-standing spiritual intertwining of minds and hearts.

Venus in hard aspect to Jupiter: Your sense of form and harmony extend into the important relationships of your life. You seek a strong philosophical connection to match your physical passion. Faithfulness is a key factor if your relationship is to support your spiritual growth, and trust has to work both ways in the partnership.

Venus in hard aspect to Saturn: You may find that your best sexual relationships are with individuals who are significantly older or younger than yourself. The role of teacher is so significant in your life that it may pervade your love life. You will need to overcome a sense of reserve or inhibition to deepen your spiritual connection.

Venus in hard aspect to Uranus: You tend to fall in love instantly, and you need to discriminate between passing sexual fancy and something that can last "forever." As your intuition develops, you will be able to identify the difference more clearly. When you "fall," that is a good time to marshal all your respect for yourself and your partner, and to take things one day at a time until you have forged a deep connection.

Venus in hard aspect to Neptune: Sexual relationships tend to arouse your idealistic nature and may have little foundation for a long-term relationship. Once past the initial stage of love, however, your imagination fuels the flame of intense spirituality and you are capable of ecstatic insights. Mystical practices can enhance your sex life.

Venus in hard aspect to Pluto: Your sexual intensity can lead you into all the wrong kinds of relationships. With a bit of judgment, however, that very intensity can set you and your partner on the path of creative expression and can stimulate bursts of spiritual consciousness. Allow time in between to integrate your experiences.

Venus in hard aspect to the Node: You tend to fall in love in some way with each person you meet, seeing the spiritual light within them and acknowledging it directly. You can surround yourself with people who share your artistic and romantic sensibilities, and also learn to adapt your capacity for love to the necessities of each situation.

Venus in hard aspect to the Asc: You have to work hard to create an environment that suits your spiritual values. Because harmony is a primary consideration in all of your activities, make it one of your spiritual considerations as well.

Venus in hard aspect to the MC: Women provide illumination of your ego so that you can become more conscious. At the same time they can challenge your core beliefs and make you aware of inconsistencies.

Mars in hard aspect to Jupiter: Your spiritual interaction with other people is generally quite fortunate in nature. You gain an understanding of a wide range of spiritual teachings through direct contact with others, and you develop the ability to resolve conflicts on all levels of your business and personal life in this way.

Mars in hard aspect to Saturn: Your involvement with other people often focuses on the harshest side of human experience. You become aware of destructive energies around you and learn to overcome these difficulties. Your spiritual life can become the source of nearly inexhaustible energy. You face tests through death or separation.

Mars in hard aspect to Uranus: Your life is peppered with dangerous intersections where you may be physically injured. These very events, however, form the substance of your spiritual path. It takes courage to follow this independent path, and effort to maintain strong relationships as you do so. Intuition can be a great asset.

Mars in hard aspect to Neptune: You are all too aware of your own weaknesses and need to develop a sure sense of your own spiritual motivation. Then relationships with others form on the established ground of inspiration and compassion. As you overcome the urge to indulge in momentary physical pleasures, you build the capacity for spiritual ecstasy.

Mars in hard aspect to Pluto: You perceive the cruel edge in people, and understand its source. As you deal with your own ruthlessness, you learn how to respond to it in others without risking your physical well-being. Self-confidence develops out of self-control in all your interactions with others.

Mars in hard aspect to the Node: You may have many relationships that never get beyond the surface physical attraction. As you learn to cooperate on the mundane issues, your astral relationships will take on emotional intensity. Then collaboration occurs on many levels of consciousness.

Mars in hard aspect to the Asc: You may experience accidents or injuries that test your spiritual values. Quarreling will not help.

Mars in hard aspect to the MC: Your biggest challenge may be to harness your own energy so that your self-awareness keeps pace with your actions. Otherwise you find yourself wondering what happened to your self-control.

Jupiter in hard aspect to Saturn: In all your business and personal dealings you have the capacity for patience. You keep one eye on the goal and the other on the moment-to-moment activities that lead you forward. You find that while relationships are significant, periods of seclusion are needed for you to integrate the spiritual changes you are experiencing.

Jupiter in hard aspect to Uranus: Your best and strongest relationships emerge from chance meetings, and you tend to depend on luck to carry you through difficult times. Your strong intuition provides insight into the almost organic rhythm of your life. Your independent spirit thrives on a less restrictive spiritual practice.

Jupiter in hard aspect to Neptune: You seek the company of visionaries, as you appreciate their ability to speculate on the future and to develop something radically new and different out of something well established. You either succumb to your impressionability and gullibility, or you learn to discern the motives that drive others and then make your own decisions.

Jupiter in hard aspect to Pluto: You seek a leadership role in all your activities, and this is equally true in your spiritual life. You first need to learn the true synthesis of love and wisdom, so that you are worthy of the faith others place in you. And you must avoid the temptation to exploit situations just because you can.

Jupiter in hard aspect to the Node: Generally you find your associations with others to be advantageous. As your spiritual awareness grows, this becomes a more consistent element of your life, until you are able to avoid or manage all contacts by evoking tact and harmony, even in one who would be your opponent.

Jupiter in hard aspect to the Asc: You are fortunate throughout your life to have discovered your inner spiritual voice. Share it with others. You may resist the spiritual values you are taught, and even argue with your teachers. This turns out to be a waste of valuable effort.

Jupiter in hard aspect to the MC: You have the capacity to develop awareness of your own love-wisdom. In your public life you find expansive, rich examples of how the laws of the universe unfold and what they mean to you. Accept the teachings, not with a sense of egotism, but with a sense of responsibility, or even duty.

Saturn in hard aspect to Uranus: Your interactions with the world are the cause of irritation and strain, and require you to develop your will to overcome difficulties. You like to maintain a particular rhythm. When this is not possible, you tend to rebel. Your spiritual understanding is tempered by your response/reaction to pressure.

Saturn in hard aspect to Neptune: You are often fully aware of the suffering of others, and tend to take it into yourself. This can make you rather moody, or it can serve to strengthen your spiritual resolve. It is important for you to sort out your own neurotic behavior before you take on the problems of others.

Saturn in hard aspect to Pluto: You can bully your way to success at the expense of the people around you, or you can learn to step outside your own ego and see the larger importance of your actions. Your strength makes you a powerful practitioner of magic, and also permits profound spiritual development in seclusion or silence.

Saturn in hard aspect to the Node: Associations with individuals much older than your-self are the stuff of your spiritual education. Examine your inhibitions (you have some), and seek to break out of your natural desire to isolate yourself.

Saturn in hard aspect to the Asc: You face major difficulties during certain periods of your life. You gain experience the hard way, and feel you are held back from success.

Saturn in hard aspect to the MC: You are more than your responsibilities. However, you are responsible for and responsive to the structure of your own life. Self-awareness can serve your spiritual development by showing how you truly feel about the things you believe you must do.

Uranus in hard aspect to Neptune: Through contact with other people, you develop an inner psychic vision. At first you dismiss your psychic insights as flukes, but later you may find that they become more frequent, more accurate, and more spiritually enriching.

Uranus in hard aspect to Pluto: Each person you meet holds the promise of transforma-tion—for you and for themselves. Your path includes the ability to facilitate change on a higher creative plane, elevating people out of their fear and sorrow. In this sense you are a very unusual agent of spiritual transmutation. You may benefit from the study of alchemy.

Uranus in hard aspect to the Node: Your capacity to share your experience forms a large part of your spiritual involvement with others. You seek new experiences that help you gain the broadest understanding of life. Your life is punctuated with sudden changes.

Uranus in hard aspect to the Asc: Sudden changes in direction have dramatic effects on your personal, social, and spiritual life. Harsh events can be the source of spiritual growth.

Uranus in hard aspect to the MC: Self-awareness comes through dramatic, sudden events. To the extent that you can foresee them intuitively, you can avoid their harsh impact to some extent.

Neptune in hard aspect to Pluto: You live on the soul level, associating every experience with your spiritual development. From time to time you are surrounded by mystics and people with strange perceptions. Sometimes obsessive, you eventually resolve confusion into self-realization.

Neptune in hard aspect to the Node: Generally you are not a strong team player. You doubt the value of cooperative effort and expect more of others than they are likely to give. Thus your efforts are better directed to self-discipline. This apparent limitation can be overcome by focusing on the stronger areas of your personality.

Neptune in hard aspect to the Asc: You need to stick to wholesome nutrition, both physical and spiritual, as you are easily swayed by drugs and by sugary words.

Neptune in hard aspect to the MC: Psychic energies bombard you and cause distress until you learn to read the messages in terms of yourself. Seek the answer within instead of projecting the message onto other people, even if you think the message is about them.

Pluto in hard aspect to the Node: Your vision focuses on the common destiny of large groups of people, and not on the day-to-day details of life. When you find yourself in the public eye, you may feel that your personal efforts have a limited effect. Look for the karmic links in your associations with others.

Pluto in hard aspect to the Asc: Use sound judgment in the use of force. Spirit guides you, but cannot always protect you against your own recklessness.

Pluto in hard aspect to the MC: You have great power to affect the world and to gain self-awareness. Even when you are using your power in your career or other areas of your life, recall the goal of spiritual self-awareness, moment to moment.

No hard aspects: I have never seen a chart without any hard aspects, nor have I seen one without any easy aspects.

The Easy Aspects
The Trine, Sextile, and Semisextile

The trine aspect divides the circle into three equal parts. The planets in a trine have a relaxed, easy relationship because they typically are in signs of the same element, and therefore compatible parts of the personality are being emphasized. Fire signs place an emphasis on your intuitive strengths. Earth signs focus on spiritual perception. Air signs indicate that thinking through spiritual issues is possible, and water signs define your emotional commitment to your spiritual path. Trines in the element of your Sun sign are often the most clearly understood, and they support your ultimate spiritual goals directly. Trines in other elements, even though closer in orb, may not express as forcefully.

To gain the benefit of trines, you need to do some work. Trines indicate conditions that exist, not actions that will occur. You have to act on the condition to gain any benefit. Trines indicate areas where you can form spiritual concepts and work with your ego instead of against it.

The sextile aspect also relates elements to each other that are considered compatible in the Western astrological system. Fire needs air to burn, and air is warmed by fire. We water the earth to grow crops, and the earth also provides a container for water. Sextiles indicate where we may find our opportunities for spiritual growth, and it is up to us to take advantage of what we find. Each of us controls our own destiny when we choose to accept this kind of opportunity. No one can do the work for us, and no one else can reap the rewards.

The semisextile links consecutive zodiacal signs, and therefore represents a natural outgrowth of one energy from another. While the elements of consecutive signs are not especially compatible, the growth process is a natural, evolutionary one. Thus the semisextile indicates an evolution on the spiritual path.

Growth does not come without some effort. With the trine, sextile, and semi-sextile, you have to identify when conditions are right for you to move forward. Traditionally these aspects are said to be easy, and the potential they offer can certainly slide by easily if you do not take action. Read the following combinations with the understanding that you must grasp each situation in order to gain any benefit.

The Sun in easy aspect to the Moon: The spiritual character you portray to the world is a comfortable reflection of the spirit within your being. You move through life with serenity born of the fact that your expression reflects your inner nature clearly.

The Sun in easy aspect to Mercury: You are able to communicate your spiritual values through your outer demeanor. When you are able to express your values through logical, reasonable words and actions, you find yourself most comfortable with your inner values.

The Sun in easy aspect to Venus: Through your daily activities you express the true beauty of spirit. You know, at the core of your being, that love and compassion are the only activities of lasting spiritual value for you.

The Sun in easy aspect to Mars: You identify with the fearlessness in yourself and others when actions are motivated by Spirit. Even physical desire, when inspired by devotion to the partner, can become a profound expression of your spirituality.

The Sun in easy aspect to Jupiter: Your good fortune, seemingly accidental in character, is more likely the consequence or effect of your aspiration to express love through wisdom, and wisdom through love. People are comfortable in your presence.

The Sun in easy aspect to Saturn: You find that spiritual discipline is as much a container for your being as it is the expression of your inner desire. Your perception of duty is to develop the endurance needed to weather emotional and material storms.

The Sun in easy aspect to Uranus: Spiritual character for you is involved in the playing out of rituals in daily activities. You have an intuitive bias toward respectful behavior, and you listen to this inner voice for guidance in difficult moments.

The Sun in easy aspect to Neptune: Psychic perception is part and parcel of your daily life. These perceptions develop into sympathy in an ordinary sense, and later into empathy for all living things. Psychic ability manifests easily once you allow it.

The Sun in easy aspect to Pluto: You are able to cut through the delusion of the material world to the heart of your spiritual power. You comprehend the continuity of your psychic states as you move between spiritual planes, and even between lives.

The Sun in easy aspect to the Midheaven: As you move through life, you find that what you know about yourself more and more closely approximates your inner spiritual being. You are able to evaluate your spiritual position with great precision.

The Sun in easy aspect to the Node: Associations with other people, and indeed with spirit animals and powerful plants, provide you with a comfortable stage on which to express your developing spiritual character. You learn from others in a natural, fluid way.

The Sun in easy aspect to the Asc: You gain recognition through others, and self-confidence through spiritual endeavors as well as public events.

The Moon in easy aspect to Mercury: The spirit within you expresses itself in the world almost without effort. Others can see the values you hold most important in your actions, hear them in your words, and therefore come to respect your opinions.

The Moon in easy aspect to Venus: The spiritual beauty that you extend into the world, through creative efforts or through facilitation of others, is a comfortable mirroring of your internal values.

The Moon in easy aspect to Mars: The spirit within you desires material expression, and you search fearlessly for the way to show how you feel to others. People find they can depend on your devotion to your principles.

The Moon in easy aspect to Jupiter: Your higher values radiate from you in the form of spiritual vision. Your actions become more and more consistent with your inner values.

The Moon in easy aspect to Saturn: Others sometimes feel you are depressed or that you place unrealistic limits on your own actions. Actually it is through such discipline that you allow your spirit to rise to the occasion when called by duty.

The Moon in easy aspect to Uranus: Your inner spirit functions easily on the intuitive plane, as you are able to identify and listen to the voice that guides your interactions with others to both their highest good and your own.

The Moon in easy aspect to Neptune: Your sympathetic nature utilizes the close connection between other people and your spiritual self. You are open to experience the joy and pain in others, and thereby grow in understanding of your own values.

The Moon in easy aspect to Pluto: Power surges around you all the time, and you find you gradually become more attuned to its currents and nuances. Your spirit guides you towards power, not for its own sake, but so that you can learn how to use it well.

The Moon in easy aspect to the Node: You feel the ebb and flow of the energy of the universe within yourself, and you perceive its flow when you are in groups of people. Focus on the flow, not the interruptions, and you will see each person's spiritual path, as well as your own.

The Moon in easy aspect to the Asc: Women inspire your spiritual life just as they influence you in other ways. Your soul and persona are well aligned. Thus other people are seldom surprised by your decisions and actions.

The Moon in easy aspect to the Midheaven: Your less conscious mental style suits what you know about yourself. You are more comfortable than most people with the paradox of being conscious while operating from a less conscious base of spiritual strength.

Mercury in easy aspect to Venus: Spirit expresses through you in the form of material creation. Whether you use words, music, or art, or simply assist others in discovering their highest expression, you are mediating between spirit and the material world each day.

Mercury in easy aspect to Mars: You become passionate when you discuss spiritual values. You don't like the feeling of anger, yet you allow it to arise when the purpose is to convince yourself or others of a spiritual necessity.

Mercury in easy aspect to Jupiter: You allow your thoughts to expand into spiritual realms without restriction, and you use this process to cleanse your mind and your words so that spirit can express ever more cleanly and clearly.

Mercury in easy aspect to Saturn: You will come to appreciate the fact that you mediate between the discipline of the spiritual path and the realities of material existence. You are able to enjoy life while communicating your spiritual values.

Mercury in easy aspect to Uranus: Intuition comes to you and you are able to express its meaning to others. The flow between ordinary words and intuitive content is smooth and natural.

Mercury in easy aspect to Neptune: Your psychic senses are tuned so that you can talk about them clearly. You develop the capacity to tell other people the oddest impressions without causing discomfort.

Mercury in easy aspect to Pluto: Powerful will stands behind your words, whether they focus on spiritual matters or mundane circumstances.

Mercury in easy aspect to the Node: You hold your own in conversation, and are a welcome guest. You are able to share your deepest thoughts and beliefs with the people around you.

Mercury in easy aspect to the Asc: Your critical nature is put to good use when you save it for essential situations and let people relax into their own strengths the rest of the time.

Mercury in easy aspect to the Midheaven: You can speak fluently about how you came to understand your spiritual journey. This is because you have had many conversations with your inner spiritual source, asking questions and sharing feelings.

Venus in easy aspect to Mars: Your creative capacity, whether it be through the arts, sexuality, or other vehicles, brings you into contact with your spirituality. Your own sensitivity can help you cultivate a more tactful nature.

Venus in easy aspect to Jupiter: Your magnetic nature attracts others to you, and you are popular without making much effort. Sharing your spiritual joy does not have to involve sharing on the physical level.

Venus in easy aspect to Saturn: Your sense of duty makes you a stable factor in difficult situations. Faithful completion of your accepted duties brings spiritual contentment into your life.

Venus in easy aspect to Uranus: On the physical level you feel the sexual spark in relationships immediately. On the spiritual level you are able to discern facts about their future through the same spark.

Venus in easy aspect to Neptune: Your receptive nature allows you to gather information from your surroundings through psychic osmosis. Study situations to get past the shallow mystical veneer.

Venus in easy aspect to Pluto: Your powerful artistic gifts can provide the media for your spiritual expression. Sometimes you are driven by a physical compulsion to produce tangible works.

Venus in easy aspect to the Node: The significant relationships in your life all share a profound loving capacity. You appreciate visual expressions of spiritual values.

Venus is easy aspect to the Asc: Your generally affectionate nature attracts both good and bad influences. You have to sort them out for yourself.

Venus in easy aspect to the Midheaven: Vanity could be a problem if your focus is on yourself. When you focus on the spiritual connections you have, you express affection to everyone you meet.

Mars in easy aspect to Jupiter: You are usually able to direct your will to productive activities. You find the transcendent component in each relationship and build on it. You exemplify joy in your daily activities.

Mars in easy aspect to Saturn: You may find that you go from one transformative situation to another, never really settling into any one thing. Yet you have the endurance necessary for the long haul.

Mars in easy aspect to Uranus: You find yourself brushing up against dangerous situations. Spiritually you learn from each one, eventually learning how to help others without taking unnecessary risks yourself.

Mars in easy aspect to Neptune: Compassion comes easily to you. The trick, if there is one, is to think through what will truly help before you leap to the rescue. Let others help themselves when they can.

Mars in easy aspect to Pluto: You are capable of applying tremendous effort to anything you attempt. The spiritual lesson is to learn moderation. Moderation often means acting like one of the pack instead of always being the leader.

Mars in easy aspect to the Node: It is important for you to maintain a consistent rhythm, including the physical, astral, and spiritual in your daily meditation. Working with others lifts you spiritually.

Mars in easy aspect to the Asc: Your fighting spirit reflects the sincerity and importance of your spiritual values. Others see you as enthusiastic, and sometimes pushy.

Mars in easy aspect to the Midheaven: You tend to act from your own spiritual center, to the extent that you understand that center. Therefore it is worth your effort to examine your career, relationships, and personal motives in every area.

Jupiter in easy aspect to Saturn: You have the capacity to endure through the daily grind to find something of spiritual value in your work and relationships. You are happy to spend time in seclusion, studying or meditating.

Jupiter in easy aspect to Uranus: You can achieve self-realization by developing your intuitive senses completely. You tend to "get the point" suddenly after careful digestion of the facts.

Jupiter in easy aspect to Neptune: You love to speculate about metaphysical or religious problems, considering both the idealistic expression of spirit and the more mundane applications of what you have learned along your path.

Jupiter in easy aspect to Pluto: You could become a charismatic leader in the spiritual arena, but your best motivation is not power. Teaching others is a better reason for rising to a leadership position.

Jupiter in easy aspect to the Node: On the practical level you value the harmonious relationships you have with others. The spiritual value lies in the capacity to form strong partnerships that support your spiritual path.

Jupiter in easy aspect to the Asc: You are fortunate throughout your life to have discovered your inner spiritual voice. Share it with others.

Jupiter in easy aspect to the Midheaven: Your have the capacity to become fully conscious of your spiritual values and the path you follow during this lifetime. You also can become content with your progress toward self-awareness.

Saturn in easy aspect to Uranus: Bad things happen. This is a fact of life that you must come to terms with. You have the spiritual depth to overcome the physical difficulties and to reach out for the spiritual intelligence behind any situation.

Saturn in easy aspect to Neptune: You understand suffering and are well able to alleviate it for others. One spiritual outcome is that you learn to accept help when you most need it yourself, thereby helping others develop compassion.

Saturn in easy aspect to Pluto: You have the self-discipline of a sorcerer or shaman. You find the smallest positive within the worst situations. You deny your own desires in order to grow mentally and spiritually.

Saturn in easy aspect to the Node: You work in isolation, and therefore need to develop strong meditation practices that cultivate the capacity to work with others who are much older or younger than yourself.

Saturn in easy aspect to the Asc: You learn to take small, careful steps on any path, but you find that a steady pace results in positive outcomes. You work well with older people.

Saturn in easy aspect to the Midheaven: You have the structure within your spirit to organize and concentrate the teachings you experience. Much of this work may take place in isolation, as it is serious personal work. You have the endurance you need for your spiritual work.

Uranus in easy aspect to Neptune: You have natural psychic ability that can express through mediumship, conscious psychic or telepathic communication and mystical interests. This needs to be balanced with physical grounding of some kind.

Uranus in easy aspect to Pluto: Your natural revolutionary zeal can conflict with a steady spiritual developmental process. You can become the founder of a new order, or burn yourself out with excessive effort in the moment.

Uranus in easy aspect to the Node: You can grasp the energy of a group and express it clearly so that everyone understands. You may have very unusual dreams that show you the best spiritual direction.

Uranus in easy aspect to the Asc: You are quick to respond, and intuition helps you find the right answers. You may upset others with your enthusiasm.

Uranus in easy aspect to the Midheaven: Your independence of mind is both the most difficult mental obstacle to overcome and the most refined mental state you can reach. This paradox occupies your thoughts and provides rich ground for spiritual development.

Neptune in easy aspect to Pluto: You are sensitive to the urgings of your inner voice, and you may even hear the voice within other people. You will experience visions and other forms of psychic awareness.

Neptune in easy aspect to the Node: You have strong compassion for others, yet you may be inconsistent in the application of effort in trying to help them. You often expect more from a situation than you get, spiritually or otherwise.

Neptune in easy aspect to the Asc: You are easily influenced by other people and need to develop your spiritual voice to counteract this tendency.

Neptune in easy aspect to the Midheaven: Your natural psychic ability provides creative imagination and bolsters your self-esteem. It also sets up the opportunity for self-doubt that in turn tests your core beliefs and allows for creative change.

Pluto in easy aspect to the Node: You find yourself concerned about the fortunes of your associates, and you seek to influence them through group activities or public office.

Pluto in easy aspect to the Asc: You can easily influence others to follow your lead, spiritual or otherwise. Be careful how you use this power.

Pluto in easy aspect to the Midheaven: You have the capacity to reshape your life into whatever you desire. In the long run you transcend base desires by recognizing power and working with it, not be trying to own it.

No easy aspects: I have never seen a chart without a trine, sextile, or semisextile. Nor have I seen one without a hard aspect.

The Creative Aspects
The Quintile, Biquintile, and Quincunx

Three additional aspects deserve consideration here: the quintile (72 degrees), the biquintile (144 degrees), and the quincunx (150 degrees). The quintile is one fifth of the circle, the biquintile is two fifths of the circle, and the quincunx spans five signs of the zodiac. I suggest that these aspects share the fact that they call forth a creative response from the spirit. The conjunctions indicate situations in which two or more energies fuse together in your life. The hard aspects indicate events and conditions in the outer environment that act on you, and the soft aspects indicate conditions where you have the choice to take action. The three aspects under consideration here demand a creative, healing, spiritually motivated response in order to be fully effective. They indicate where your talents and skills—all of them—may be brought to bear to respond to crises or to make spiritual decisions.

As far as I know, no other astrologer has grouped these three aspects together in this way. Generally the quintile and biquintile are said to indicate talents and creative skills, while the quincunx indicates areas of expansion or adjustment in one's life and often signals an injury or illness. Perhaps it was my personal response to a near-death experience that has led me to understand the connection of creative mind in this way. My doctors told me that there had been little they could do at first except wait for me to make an effort, and I understand that effort to be a creative decision. Later I studied the work of shamans in a variety of cultures, and I realized that their initiations all shared two things. They face a death to their previous life, and that adjustment provides an opening of their creative energy.

The Sun in creative aspect to the Moon: There is a direct link between conscious and less conscious parts of your psyche that allows you to formulate spiritual goals and to move toward them.

The Sun in creative aspect to Mercury: You communicate your spiritual will clearly and creatively. Listening is a big part of this ability.

The Sun in creative aspect to Venus: You see the harmony in all things, even when there is distress around you. This helps you manifest solutions quickly.

The Sun in creative aspect to Mars: You create best on the energetic level, working with the present energy levels and moving to a higher level.

The Sun in creative aspect to Jupiter: You move easily into new creative ventures, sure of yourself and your ability to find the proper expression of your ideas.

The Sun in creative aspect to Saturn: You take responsibilities seriously and use your intelligence to make appropriate changes.

The Sun in creative aspect to Uranus: You glimpse the future moments, days, or even weeks before it becomes reality. This vision provides the basis for creative action.

The Sun in creative aspect to Neptune: You sense the physical, emotional, and spiritual rhythms of the world around you and use them in your daily activities.

The Sun in creative aspect to Pluto: You are able to manipulate the power in the world around you to create what you need and desire, for yourself and for others.

The Sun in creative aspect to the Node: You can take the energy of a group and meld it into a creative force. Spiritually this can translate into more powerful results than the individuals could accomplish alone.

The Sun in creative aspect to the Asc: You join your self and your public persona in all your activities. You are trusted as a source of spiritual stability.

The Sun in creative aspect to the MC: The more you come to understand yourself, the better your creative will can express on the spiritual level.

The Moon in creative aspect to Mercury: Your inner voice expresses through your physical voice, so this talent needs to be developed.

The Moon in creative aspect to Venus: Love is a medium of expression for you—this can be through physical relationships, mental activities, or spiritual communion.

The Moon in creative aspect to Mars: You choose an independent, unusual path for your creative expression. In this way the inner voice can best be heard.

The Moon in creative aspect to Jupiter: You balance love and wisdom that comes from a source deep within you to create spiritually inspired works.

The Moon in creative aspect to Saturn: You take your creative process very seriously. You listen carefully to your inner voice and then try to manifest the desired effect in everything you do.

The Moon in creative aspect to Uranus: If there is real pixie dust on the world, you have some of it! Your creative efforts feel completely natural, yet magical.

The Moon in creative aspect to Neptune: The only illusion about your creative process is that you seem to produce results from thin air. Actually, they come from your close connection to your spirit.

The Moon in creative aspect to Pluto: As a child you thought that if a little red was good, a lot was a whole lot better. You have learned that sometimes less is more, especially where spirit is concerned.

The Moon in creative aspect to the Node: Your associates don't live in your mind, but their ideas provide fuel for your own creative efforts. Your inner voice needs others for the best effect.

The Moon in creative aspect to the Asc: Your subconscious mind is a rich source of spiritual information that guides your relationships with women and with the public.

The Moon in creative aspect to the MC: The balance of self-awareness and the inner voice is strong in your life. Each nurtures the other.

Mercury in creative aspect to Venus: Expression of the beauty you perceive in the world can take many forms. When interwoven with spiritual values, it is even more elegant.

Mercury in creative aspect to Mars: Verbal expression of spiritual values comes naturally to you. You may even become zealous in your efforts to convert others to your point of view.

Mercury in creative aspect to Jupiter: Philosophical ideas and discussions help you form your creative plans—such conversations expand the boundaries of your own thinking.

Mercury in creative aspect to Saturn: There is a time for serious conversations in the creative process. You tend to provide the thoughtful content that makes projects reach their higher potential.

Mercury in creative aspect to Uranus: Intuition inspires your creative activities. You try new things on a whim and hold on to the methods that work well for you.

Mercury in creative aspect to Neptune: Spiritual values flow through you from the universe to others. No application of force is necessary or desirable.

Mercury in creative aspect to Pluto: A forceful communication style is your hallmark. Practice your verbal skills so that you get the most creative bang from each conversation.

Mercury in creative aspect to the Node: Your creative efforts achieve the best results when they are supported by group activity, based on shared spiritual values.

Mercury in creative aspect to the Asc: You use your critical abilities to enhance your work and to enliven your speech.

Mercury in creative aspect to the MC: Self-knowledge guides your creativity and therefore you will come back to personal considerations frequently.

Venus in creative aspect to Mars: Love is your best creative medium. This means that romantic partnerships, sexual fulfillment, and spiritual communion all can be used to develop creatively.

Venus in creative aspect to Jupiter: You reach for the philosophical expression of love in your life, not satisfied with momentary physical release.

Venus in creative aspect to Saturn: Self-control can put a damper on your creative expression. Develop a structure for your work, then learn to use inhibition as a tool.

Venus in creative aspect to Uranus: You fall in and out of love at the drop of a hat. Let this tendency express itself in your creative activities and it will add spiritual spice.

Venus in creative aspect to Neptune: Use erotic fantasies to fuel spiritual expression. Religious art demonstrates that you are not the first to do so.

Venus in creative aspect to Pluto: You are artistically gifted. Use your powers of attraction to draw a strong mix of people into your life to enrich your spirit.

Venus in creative aspect to the Node: Your creative talents are adaptable to any situation, and that includes your spiritual path.

Venus in creative aspect to the Asc: You have a talent for decorating, flower arranging, or other artistic efforts that can inspire your spiritual development.

Venus in creative aspect to the MC: Spiritual creativity thrives in a harmonious environment. Use your creative abilities to develop the right space for your work.

Mars in creative aspect to Jupiter: You probably have more creative ideas than you know what to do with. Learn to identify the ideas that will carry you toward your spiritual goal, and let the others go.

Mars in creative aspect to Saturn: Even in death there is a creative aspect. You are the master of finding the gems to save after a storm has destroyed just about everything.

Mars in creative aspect to Uranus: Break the mold if you must, but keep the casting that is the product of your intuitive activity.

Mars in creative aspect to Neptune: Compassion drives your creative activity. Don't spend any time on projects that are not guided by this higher principle.

Mars in creative aspect to Pluto: You are able to work all situations to your advantage. If you press a bit more lightly, you may find that the subtle results are better.

Mars in creative aspect to the Node: How to be creative while working within a group—that is your question. Begin by taking on one small piece of the project and doing it as well as you possibly can.

Mars in creative aspect to the Asc: Use your energy in creative projects that reflect your inner spiritual values.

Mars in creative aspect to the MC: You know better than anyone how your energy complements or interferes with your spiritual goals. Listen to yourself.

Jupiter in creative aspect to Saturn: You can handle grand strategies or the little details, because you understand the relationship between structure and process.

Jupiter in creative aspect to Uranus: Your creative energy runs in spurts—on again, off again. Through intuitive planning you can be prepared when it is on again.

Jupiter in creative aspect to Neptune: As you move along the spiritual path, your compassion is guided more and more by wisdom born from past creative efforts.

Jupiter in creative aspect to Pluto: Expand your own creative horizons. Avoid narrowing your vision to include only forceful control over the creativity of others.

Jupiter in creative aspect to the Node: Group activity has a fortunate effect on your creativity, as you absorb concepts from the group and apply them to your own spiritual model.

Jupiter in creative aspect to the Asc: You can use your sense of spiritual harmony in every part of your creative process. Let the light shine in your words.

Jupiter in creative aspect to the MC: Each creative activity allows you to expand your self-awareness in some way. You are fortunate to have the ability to see the continuity of your efforts clearly.

Saturn in creative aspect to Uranus: Early in life you listen to your elders to develop creative skill. Later you will share your talents with younger people.

Saturn in creative aspect to Neptune: Your capacity to use compassion constructively places you in a responsible position. Use your knowledge to help others and you will find you move toward your own spiritual goals.

Saturn in creative aspect to Pluto: Perhaps your hardest lesson in the creative sphere is that pushing too hard is more likely to break things than to produce satisfying results.

Saturn in creative aspect to the Node: Be responsible to others, but more than that, be responsive to the ideas and feelings of others. Herein lies your creative skill.

Saturn in creative aspect to the Asc: Your deep understanding of the structure of your personality and of the world is the key to creative activities. You know how things work on both the physical and spiritual planes.

Saturn in creative aspect to the MC: Listen to the voice of the Old Man or Old Woman that comes from within you. Your connection to the past—even ancient history—reveals spiritual meaning now.

Uranus in creative aspect to Neptune: Profound awareness of the world around you on the psychic level is paired with intuition concerning the future. Together they make for a highly creative package.

Uranus in creative aspect to Pluto: You create whole new ways of living through your deep connection to the earth and to other sentient beings.

Uranus in creative aspect to the Node: While variety makes your life more exciting, your spiritual path is one of equilibrium. Create an environment in which you can experience both.

Uranus in creative aspect to the Asc: You have an uncanny inner guidance system that helps your creative efforts. Spiritual intuition is strong.

Uranus in creative aspect to the MC: Intuition guides your creative activities, showing you possible outcomes. Use this information to make clear choices.

Neptune in creative aspect to Pluto: Your psychic awareness allows you to guide the activities of groups wisely and creatively, without the use of force of will.

Neptune in creative aspect to the Node: Group activities disappoint you only when you rely on the creativity of others instead of your own sense of what will work.

Neptune in creative aspect to the Asc: Use your natural compassion to expand and refine your creative efforts. In this way others benefit not only from your actions, but also by understanding your values.

Neptune in creative aspect to the MC: Psychic awareness enhances your self-awareness, and thus enables you to act more creatively in most situations.

Pluto in creative aspect to the Node: You are able to find and encourage associations with other people to foster creative spiritual growth for yourself and for them.

Pluto in creative aspect to the Asc: Personal power is a force for good in your life. Use it to expound on key spiritual values.

Pluto in creative aspect to the MC: You are able to use the power inherent in your environment to transform yourself and others spiritually.

No creative aspects: I have never seen a chart without any creative aspects.

CONCLUSION

I would like to summarize by going back to the beginning of this book. I mentioned a number of spiritual goals, describing them as avenues to your higher purpose in this lifetime. Chapter 12 on the Ascendant includes a statement of how you can choose to express your spiritual values in a direct way through your persona, or personality. The principal ways you can express your values, and assist others in attaining their higher purpose as well, are these:

1. Intelligent activity

2. Finding harmony through conflict

3. Gathering and using concrete knowledge

4. Awakening to the spiritual in everything

5. Finding ways to join wisdom and love in your life

6. Pursuing a life of effective action, through skillful means

7. Perceiving and cultivating equilibrium

8. Psychic awareness

9. Cultivation of compassion for yourself and others

10. Using your own power and will to do the best you can every day

The chapters of this book are organized around the planets, the Midheaven, and the Ascendant. These fundamental building blocks of the astrological chart reflect your potential for building on all the past history that led to your birth, in order to reach for spiritual understanding. They show how you can take action each day, in one or more areas of your life, to cultivate an environment that suits your spiritual needs. They reveal your personal perspective on life. They offer suggestions about how you can enrich your life and help others at the same time.

None of us are likely to achieve perfection in any of the ten areas listed here. However, all of us can use the spiritual picture that astrology provides to feel more content with life, more satisfied that we are good people, and more joyous that we contribute to the happiness and well-being of others.

THE HEART SUTRA

Homage to the Perfection of Wisdom, the Lovely, the Holy!

Avalokita, The Holy Lord and Bodhisattva, was moving in the deep course of the Wisdom which has gone beyond.

He looked down from on high, he beheld but five heaps, and he saw that in their own-being they were empty.

Here, O Sariputra, form is emptiness and the very emptiness is form; emptiness does not differ from form, form does not differ from emptiness; whatever is form, that is emptiness, whatever is emptiness, that is form, the same is true of feelings, perceptions, impulses, and consciousness.

Here, O Sariputra, all dharmas are marked with emptiness; they are not produced or stopped, not defiled or immaculate, not deficient or complete.

Therefore, O Sariputra, in emptiness there is no form, nor feeling, nor perception, nor impulse, nor consciousness; No eye, ear, nose, tongue, body, mind; No forms, sounds, smells, tastes, touchables or objects of mind; No sight-organ element, and so forth, until we come to: No mind-consciousness element; There is no ignorance, no extinction of ignorance, and so forth, until we come to: there is no decay and death, no extinction of decay and death. There is no suffering, no origination, no stopping, no path. There is no cognition, no attainment and no non-attainment.

Therefore, O Sariputra, it is because of his non-attainmentness that a Bodhisattva, through having relied on the perfection of wisdom, dwells without thought-coverings. In the absence of thought-coverings he has not been made to tremble, he has overcome what can upset, and in the end he attains to Nirvana.

Therefore one should know the prajnaparamita as the great spell, the spell of great knowledge, the utmost spell, the unequalled spell, allayer of all suffering, in truth—for what could go wrong? By the prajnaparamita has this spell been delivered. It runs like this:

Gone, gone, gone beyond, gone altogether beyond, O what an awakening, all-hail!

—This completes the Heart of perfect wisdom.

GLOSSARY

Auras: "The human aura is a developmental, life-sustaining energy force that characterizes every human being . . . Under appropriate conditions, the aura can be seen by almost everyone . . . The aura is sensitive to the totality of our inner and outer environment . . . The human aura is never without color . . . The aura is a visible manifestation of the life force that energizes our total being—mentally, physically, and spiritually." (Slate, *Aura Energy for Health, Healing & Balance*)

Chakras: "The chakras are spinning vortexes of subtle energy located along the spine from the base to the crown. Each of the seven main chakras offers a different perspective on life or any given situation . . . The energy of the chakras, although subtle rather than physical, permeates all aspects of your life." (Pond, *Chakras for Beginners*, 5–7)

Clairaudience: "Clairaudience is the receiving of sounds and voices of a psychic nature. Spiritualists often rely on clairaudience in order to receive messages from the spirit world. People who channel messages from higher realms are also employing clairaudience in many cases." (Grimassi, *Encyclopedia of Wicca & Witchcraft*, 77)

Clairvoyance: "Clairvoyance is the receiving of mental impressions or images of a psychic nature. This is commonly referred to as 'being psychic.' Someone who is clarvoyant can see events taking place at a distant location and foretell future events." (Grimassi, *Encyclopedia of Wicca & Witchcraft*, 77)

Dharma: "The Hindu accepts that Dharma, or duty, is an inescapable part of living . . . When we are born, not only do we have a collective Dharma to the community at large, but also we have a personal Dharma or Swadharma. . . . The biggest single cause of frustration and unhappiness is the failure to fulfill your own Swadharma [duty to yourself]." (Mumford, *Karma Manual*, 5)

Dowsing: The use of a pendulum, metal rod, or forked stick to locate water, metals, or other objects hidden underground.

Feng Shui: "Feng Shui is the art of living in harmony with the earth . . . The words feng shui mean 'wind and water.'" (Webster, *Feng Shui for the Workplace*, 1) The people of China developed feng shui as an organized system of arranging their homes and lives to suit the energy of the earth (ch'i).

Karma: "Karma, or the Law of Karma, is an opportunity to make our lives one creative journey from womb to tomb. In fact Karma is not destiny, Karma is also free will, and in a sense it is up to us." (Mumford, *Karma Manual*, 21) Karma is a cycle of events, related by cause and effect. Past events produced karma which we may experience now, and present events produce future karma, or results.

Kundalini: "A residue of energy said to be locked within the body . . . (literally 'coiled,' implying the power inherent in a compressed spring). Certain techniques will release Kundalini up a central psychic tube (equivalent of a fluid-filled cavity, the canalis centralis, in the center of the . . . spinal cord." (Mumford, *Ecstasy Through Tantra*, 27)

Ley Lines: "Ley lines are believed to be streams of energy associated with currents that are connected to topography . . . Ley lines are associated with magnetic currents within the earth. It is held that the sun and moon influence these currents, along with the seasonal shifts marked by solstice and equinox." (Grimassi, *Encyclopedia of Wicca & Witchcraft*, 221–2)

Magic(k): "Magick is the art and metaphysical science of manifesting personal desires through the collection and direction of energy . . . Essentially magick is believed to work in several different ways. From an occult perspective, like attracts like, and therefore symbols and images of a desired object or situation can draw the goal of a spell or work of magick." (Grimassi, *Encyclopedia of Wicca & Witchcraft*, 232)

Persona: The face that you choose to show to the world, including physical appearance, personality, and actions.

Psychokinesis (telekinesis): A movement of physical objects by the mind without use of physical means; the apparent production of motion in objects without contact or other physical means.

Tantra: "Tantra is a spiritual science involving 'methods of going into the subconscious mind and diving deep into the unconscious mind . . . to clear up your personality, your deep-rooted complexes, going to correct your behavior, is going to rehabilitate you psychologically, and physically." (Mumford, *Ecstasy Through Tantra*, xiii)

BIBLIOGRAPHY

Books

Bailey, Alice. *Esoteric Astrology*. New York, NY: Lucis Publishing Company, 1951.

Conze, Edward, trans. *Buddhist Wisdom Books Containing The Diamond Sutra and The Heart Sutra*. New York, NY: Harper Torchbooks, 1958.

Doane, Doris Chase. *Horoscopes of the U.S. Presidents*. Hollywood, CA: Professional Astrologers, Inc., 1952.

Ebertin, Reinhold. *The Combination of Stellar Influences*. Aalen, Germany: Ebertin Verlag, 1972.

Grell, Paul. *Key Words*. Washington, D.C.: American Federation of Astrologers, 1970.

Grimassi, Raven. *Encyclopedia of Wicca & Witchcraft*. St. Paul, MN: Llewellyn Publications, 2000.

Mumford, Jonn. *Ecstasy Through Tantra*. St. Paul, MN: Llewellyn Publications, 1995.

———. *Karma Manual*. St. Paul, MN: Llewellyn Publications, 1999.

Penfield, Marc. *2001: The Penfield Collection*. Seattle, WA: Vulcan Books, 1979.

Pond, David. *Chakras for Beginners*. St. Paul, MN: Llewellyn Publications, 1999.

Slate, Joe H. *Aura Energy for Health, Healing & Balance*. St. Paul, MN: Llewellyn Publications, 1999.

Webster, Richard. *Feng Shui for the Workplace*. St. Paul, MN: Llewellyn Publications, 1998.

Internet Websites

www.nationalgeographic.com/faces/ali/html. Muhammad Ali website.

Astrological Computer Software

Rodden, Lois. AstroDatabank Software. Manchester, MA: 1999.

INDEX

For readers of

Charting Your Spiritual Path with Astrology

only

FREE Natal Chart Offer

Thank you for purchasing *Charting Your Spiritual Path with Astrology*. There are a number of ways to construct a chart wheel. The easiest way, of course, is by computer, and that's why we are giving you this one-time offer of a free natal chart. This extremely accurate chart will provide you with a great deal of information about yourself. Once you receive a chart from us, *Charting Your Spiritual Path with Astrology* will provide everything you need to know to use the information your chart provides as a spiritual road map.

Also, by ordering your free chart, you will be enrolled in Llewellyn's Birthday Club! From now on, you can get any of Llewellyn's astrology reports for 25% off when you order within one month of your birthday! Just write "Birthday Club" on your order form or mention it when ordering by phone. As if that wasn't enough, we will mail you a FREE copy of our fresh new book *What Astrology Can Do for You!* Go for it!

Complete this form with your accurate birth data and mail it to us today. Enjoy your adventure in self-discovery through astrology!

Do not photocopy this form. Only this original will be accepted.

Please Print

Full Name:_____

Mailing Address:_____

City, State, Zip:_____

Birth time:_____ A.M. P.M. (please circle)

Month:_____ Day:_____ Year:_____

Birthplace (city, county, state, country):

_____

_____

Check your birth certificate for the most accurate information.

Complete and mail this form to: Llewellyn Publications, Special Chart Offer, P.O. Box 64383, 0-7387-0114-9, St. Paul, MN 55164.

Allow 4–6 weeks for delivery.